The Adventures of Mack and Myndie

10 Life Lessons I Learned from My Pets

Dr. Joan Weathersbee Ellason

The Adventures of Mack and Myndie: 10 Life Lessons I Learned from My Pets

Dr. Joan Weathersbee Ellason

Copyright © 2025 Oasis Workshops with Dr. Joan Weathersbee Ellason

All Rights Reserved.

No part of this publication may be reproduced, distributed, or transmitted in any form or by any means, including photocopying, recording, or other electronic or mechanical methods, without the prior written permission

from the author, except in the case of brief quotations embodied in critical reviews and certain noncommercial uses permitted by copyright law.

Some scriptures taken from THE HOLY BIBLE, NEW INTERNATIONAL VERSION® NIV® Copyright © 1973, 1978, 1984, by International Bible Society®, 2011 by Biblica Inc®. Used with permission. All rights reserved worldwide.

The information given in this book should not be treated as a substitute for professional medical or clinical advice; always consult a medical or clinical practitioner. Any use of information in this book is at the reader's discretion and risk. Neither the author nor the publisher can be held responsible for any loss, claim, or damage arising out of the use or misuse of the suggestions made, the failure to take medical or clinical advice, or for any material on third-party websites.

First Printing: 2025

ISBN: 978-1-7357627-8-4

Dr. Joan Weathersbee Ellason

Address: 1809 K Avenue

Plano Texas 75074, U.S.A.

Tel. (469) 831-4548

Email: DrJWE@outlook.com

www.drjwe.com

Speaking Engagements

Joan Weathersbee Ellason, Ph.D., LPC, is a licensed professional counselor. As a private practice therapist since the 1990s, a workshop provider, a trauma mental health worker since the 1980s, and a research contributor to psychological, psychiatric, and pastoral counseling journals, she presents a unique and creative approach to overcoming challenges in life. She teaches groups online about methods of forgiveness, moving past trauma, and reaching for one's own personal potential.

Dr. Weathersbee Ellason is available to provide workshops on forgiveness or other topics.

For booking information:

Call or text (469) 831-4548

Email: DrJWE@outlook.com and include WORKSHOP in the subject line.

TABLE OF CONTENTS

Chapter One 1
   The Gift of Unconditional Love

Chapter Two 7
   Don't Be Afraid to Feel and to Express Your Needs

Chapter Three 15
   Expect to Be Wanted And Included

Chapter Four 27
   Embrace Joy and Play

Chapter Five 37
   Don't Ever Think You Are Too Small to Have a Big Voice

Chapter Six 49
   Know Your Power

Chapter Seven 61
   Don't Be So Mesmerized by the Prize That You Fall for Hidden Sneaky Lies

Chapter Eight 83
   Don't Be Afraid or Intimidated by Bullies

Chapter Nine 99
   Choose What Is Good for You

Chapter Ten 111
   Don't Be Afraid to Try Again—to Love Again

Chapter One

The Gift of Unconditional Love

Blessings They Can Bring

I truly wish that I had known so much more about the blessings that animals bring to us when I was younger and busier. It was not until after I had taken an elderly friend named Kay under my wing that I learned how to better attend to and understand them. She had poodles through the years and one rescue terrier, all of whom she indulged as if they were her special children. Through her example, I began to learn insights into the needs and apparent emotional experiences of these precious little beings. In many of their stories, I also realize retrospectively the wisdom that they can teach us. These chapters, looking back through their lives, will provide a glimpse of insights and wisdom that we can all learn and apply to our lives in some important ways. It is with honor that I now share them with you.

Think back to some of the pets that you have had in the past—or perhaps have currently. Even the ones with the most challenging habits may provide an often overlooked blessing. Do you agree? If not, think back to times when that amazing boyfriend or girlfriend, by whom you were mesmerized, was about to come over. You know, the one you spent hours cleaning the house or apartment for in a frenzy? You know, the one who may have later betrayed you or dumped you, even though you tried so hard to impress them, made painstaking efforts to ensure that you looked great, and put on your most alluring fragrance and outfit. At least when the relationship was new, you poured tons of energy into each encounter.

Now, switch the scene in your home to times you have been with your pet. The unconditional permissions from these forgiving little beings go on into infinity. The laundry can be piled sky-high with mess all around. Your pet doesn't notice—doesn't even care what you look like, whether the house is in order, or if there's a stench coming from your three-day-worn T-shirt. Regardless, they want to jump up on the couch beside you and snuggle next to you or just have you near them in the same room.

During the later years of life, a pet can be that companion who is by Your side after the children have launched from the nest. They can sometimes fill a void as the adult children rightfully make their own way in the world with their now busy lives. It can warm your heart when your pet shows excitement to see you when you come home, want to spend time with you , and be glad you are there.

A Unique Kind of Love

Yes, this is the ultimate in unconditional acceptance. Your wardrobe and hair can look like a dumpster fire, and your clothes can be rags and halfway falling off your body. Nevertheless, they still see you as if you are that gorgeous beauty or handsome hero you had previously strained to become for that human. You can slouch on that couch, let it all hang out, belch loudly, and even exude the strangest, most offensive sounds and odors with your hair looking like something from outer space. To them, you are still the greatest thing in their whole world. You don't have to perform for them. You don't have to impress them at all. Pets are those unique and special little beings who love you just as you are—for the very one you are. A colleague of mine stated it well. He said, "I believe that dogs (pets) with whom we develop the deepest attachment and bond are the closest example of the profound perfection of God's love we can experience in this life" (Jason Branson, personal communication, June 4, 2025).

A wise friend said, "A pet can sometimes love you even better than a parent does, in many ways" (Vanessa Mateer, personal communication, May 16, 2025). This is because they never ask, "Why did you make that [financial, career, relationship, or other personal] decision?" They never criticize or judge you. They only accept you. You can be remiss and wake up the next day with regrets, and they forgive you immediately—no questions asked. One of my favorite mentors, Dr. William Ickes, Distinguished Professor of Psychology at UTA in Arlington (personal communication, 1996), said, "To a dog, every day is a new day." The implication of that phrase is that, "the dog's forgetting goes a long way toward explaining why they are so willing to forgive us. [They] are less likely to hold grudges." (Dr. William Ickes, personal communication

September 25. 2025). It is a blessing to have a friend who does not remember our mistakes, nor hold grudges. With so many of our pets, we get to start all over again, every day, again and again.

Treasuring Our Time with Them

They are with us for such a short period of time. My sister, Judy K. Melton, says that she believes that they do go to Heaven and that we will be able to see them again one day. I hope this is true. She cites Isaiah 11:6-9 (NIV), and Isaiah 65:25 (NIV) as assurance.

After starting the outline of this book, knowing that my two 14-year-old dogs may not live to be 100, complications developed with the little brown mini pinscher that you see on the front cover. She had just been diagnosed with diabetes, and I had been frantically taking care of her needs—special foods, insulin shots twice per day, and other medications added to her already prescribed heart pills. Two weeks into this protocol, an X-ray at an emergency animal clinic revealed that she had just begun to go into heart failure and her lungs had become filled with fluid, not to mention her arthritis in her limbs, despite her additional acupuncture and chiropractic vet care previously in place. She had been suffering silently, patiently without a single complaint, always grateful for the attention and care given to her.

When the decision to say goodbye became indisputable—a decision I always hate because it feels as if you are playing God—I struggled with the aftercare post-life options. During the days after, I moved at a slower pace, and so did Mack (the black and white Boston terrier you also see on the front cover of this book, who had been with her for thirteen of his fourteen years). It is important to pace yourself and to give yourself all the time that you need to savor that loved one, embrace their memory, and take care of yourself while grieving.

The first day, I remained stunned and numb while they kindly gave me time to decide on the best afterlife plans for her. Two days later, I perceived myself to be handling it, thinking, *I'm okay, I'm okay.* Then I put the coffee pod in the machine, filled it with water, and brewed my coffee while doing other things. After a few minutes, I discovered that I had brewed the coffee without placing my cup underneath.

This book is written to honor those little precious ones, those sweet fur babies, who grace our lives with their love for such brief encounters. It is also written to give you, the pet parent, owner, pet human, permission to take all the time you need to heal. It is hoped that I can help you understand and glean from these pages the blessings and unconditional love that are meant to remain in our hearts forever while they are still here with us.

Chapter Two

Don't Be Afraid to Feel and to Express Your Needs

After my childhood dog Skipper passed away, I decided not to have any more pets. I believed that my full-time career and multiple work avenues would not allow me to supply the amount of attention needed and deserved by such a beloved little being anyway. Dogs especially need companionship.

Out of the blue, my young adult son received the cutest, tiniest little Boston terrier puppy from his father, who he named Mack. He had just been weaned, and I watched as he scampered around on the floor as my son played guitar. My son was a good, responsible pet owner. He took him out into the backyard frequently to potty train him. Mack was so tiny that the short blades of grass were taller than his whole body, and they engulfed him as he attempted to do his business.

Back inside the house, he would scamper around and nap, then wake up and scamper some more. As Mack frolicked around on the living room floor, he suddenly laid eyes on a small foot-high statue of a dinosaur towering over him from the hearth of the fireplace. Mack suddenly jumped into a startled, frozen stance staring up at it, as if a bolt of lightning had jolted through him. I marveled at what this must have felt like for Mack, bouncing around, carefree, suddenly encountering such a tall, ominously strange being. After a minute, when it did not move or respond, Mack figured out that it must not be a live being, and he resumed his playful romp. Mack was tiny enough to hold in the palm of your hand. How could I NOT fall in love with him!

About a year or so after, my son realized that he was not able to give enough quality time to this dog because of his work hours. It hurt his heart to have to leave Mack cooped up all day in his room at the house that he shared with roommates while he worked for eight/ten hours.

Shortly after that they both came to stay temporarily in my home while my son was changing his living arrangements. Mack had already bonded with my son and was beginning to bond with me as well. My son wisely did not want Mack to have to spend time alone for hours, waiting for people to get off from work, so he had found a friend who had other dogs and was willing to take him.

Once my son made this decision to give him away, it was clear that it was already impacting Mack. Without a word, Mack sensed that something was different. I broke away from my work demands for a moment, and I was struck by how this sensitive little creature was experiencing the change in the air. While my son was in his room down the hall, Mack was sitting on a sofa chair alone. I saw Mack's tears streaming down his little face, flowing all the way down, saturating his white furry chest. I have never seen a dog look so sad and so hurt. It was a stark picture of deep abandonment that I could not bear. This clutched my heart. It seemed like Mack was sensing the impending separation, wondering what was about to happen to him. What must have been going through his mind? *Why don't they want me anymore? Did I do something wrong? What is wrong with me? Am I bad?*

As the thick stream of tears continued to flow, drenching Mack's face and his chest, I marched into my son's room and told him to go get him and hold him, that he was feeling abandoned and rejected. I further asserted that I would take him in and take care of him, that I could not bear to see him at barely over a year old, feeling such devastation. My son protested that I work a lot as well, and the dog would still feel neglected. However, I was working from home which would allow me to be attentive to him. I assured him that I would also find a good dog companion for him so, while I was busy at the desk, he would have a close friend—someone to play with and to love.

My son finally acquiesced to my persistence. I did just as I had promised. Mack and I made several visits to the nearby animal shelter. Mack met and interacted with several different dogs until we found the perfect match for him. She was a small brown mini pinscher with skinny little legs. On the playground they approached each other with curious introductions, then began to play with a rhythm that was perfectly in sync. They clicked. Thus began the Adventures of Mack and Myndie.

* * *

Don't Be Afraid to Show Your Feelings

It broke my heart to see the dog so hurt. If Mack had not shed those honest and transparent tears that day, I would never have become aware of what was going on right in front of me. I would have continued cluelessly in my busy little whirlwind and not even taken a minute to have a glimpse into what was going on in this little being's heart and mind. While I had envisioned a future only filled with my work and career now that my son was grown, this introduced an unanticipated yet welcomed interruption to those plans. The weight of love outweighed my ambitions, as it had when I was raising my son as well. Now I was willing to consider a slight alteration to my rigid plans. Carving an opening in my life to allow for this little being to have a place where he knows that he is valued and loved became a priority. This was no longer an interruption and became an expansion to my plans. Taking care of him and his companion, Myndie, has brought an unexpected blessing into my life for the past thirteen years.

Sometimes it is necessary to speak up and to show someone how you really feel. Don't assume that they know without you telling them. People cannot read our minds, nor we theirs. Speak up and let people know how you feel and what you need. This is not selfish. It gives people an opportunity to do the right thing and make better choices in connection with your relationship. It presents them with an opportunity for expansion and enhancement of your bond with them. If they are a good friend, they will come through with what they can or clarify with you why they can't. If they are not willing to consider your needs at all, then you gain valuable information on whether they get to remain among your closest confidants and in your inner circle of people.

Withholding our true and honest feelings, needs, and wants often leads to a disservice to others more than we realize. How many times have you seen someone fail to speak up or express how they truly feel about an issue, only to end up eventually leaving that relationship, job, or situation in frustration? People who are truly good for you and sincerely do care about you will benefit more by your sharing this information with them than if you suffer in silence, only to leave later.

How to Speak Up

You can start by telling them what you like and appreciate about what they are doing. Then attach the word "and" (not "but," "however," or "nevertheless") to your request. Tell them what is good about what they *are* doing, then say *"and,"* followed by "I need for you to _____, or I would love it if you will _____." You may be pleasantly surprised at how they may respond when you word it as simply a request or just emotionally neutral, logical information and not a criticism. You can reiterate to them that this is not a criticism and that they are a good person, that you just want to let them know what you need because you value the relationship. If they refuse, then you also have important information that you needed to know about them anyway. It is never wrong to ask for what you need. You can ask, and they are free to say "No."

Why Speak Up

When you dare to impose an interruption (and opportunity for expansion) by speaking up, you create an opportunity for an enhancement in the other person's life. Benefits to the other person are the following:

1. You are giving them an opening to make a positive choice.
2. You create for them an opportunity for an expansion in their life.
3. You invite them to look outside themselves.
4. You offer them an option, which they are free to refuse, that can become a blessing for them if they accept.

If you do not speak up and let them know that you are bothered, uncomfortable, or hurting about something, they may not ever know, nor be able to correct that wrong. Besides, you may not ever get the chance to find that they may not have intended to hurt you at all. Many relationships become wasted by this lack of communication. Your feedback can be delivered without condemning them. It is best when carrying a tone of acceptance with how much you value the relationship.

Chapter Three

Expect to Be Wanted And Included

So the story began. When I first found Myndie at the local animal shelter that day, Mack and I were walking down one of the hallways displaying rows and rows of potential pets. This shelter was impressively clean, and the pets were placed in rooms, not cages. Each room was spacious with an upper glass window, allowing potential adoptive people to peer down from above to see them in their comfortable environments.

Halfway down one of the hallways, my attention was completely fixed on one of the rooms. A little brown mini pinscher was jumping up and down in the air, over and over again. With her little skinny, twig-like legs, she was able to propel herself high enough to look out through her own window, which was shoulder-high to me, to see the people walking by. I had never seen a dog jump that high. She had a rhythmic bounce as if her legs had springs and would catapult up repeatedly. It was like she was trying to get the upper hand by having the first glimpse of all those curious humans who would be gawking at her. She was going to be the one to gawk first. I stopped and watched her through the glass window of her room that day as she bounded up and down in a rhythmic cadence, as if she was saying, *"Pick me. Pick me. Pick me."* She was so small yet so demonstrative, jumping five times her height. That day, since I did not yet know what breed she was, I began to call her the "jumpin' chihuahua."

With Mack on the leash, we stopped to watch as her exuberance continued. With each bounce you could almost greet her at eye level as she refused to go unnoticed and was determined to figure out her strange surroundings. She seemed to be a dog that would be a promising companion for Mack during my long work hours. While I interpreted her relentless jumping as her saying, *"Pick me. Pick Me,"* in retrospect, I think she actually picked *us*!

The process of selecting a pet involved a meet and greet on the property playground. So, we asked the attendant to let Mack interact with her on their fenced-in lawn. Right away they clicked. They joined with each other in a frolicking dance that seemed perfectly choreographed. They wrapped each other with their front paws, gently wrestled and tumbled, periodically stopped to take breaks, and then they started back at it again. She was the one! We adopted her, and I named her Myndie.

Myndie had been found living on the streets as a stray. She was about one year and four months old, and due to whatever length of time she had been out there, she had learned several survival skills. She seemed to have a philosophy of "look out for number one" and was initially not quick to bond with people. This seemed to make sense for an early life of surviving on one's own. In order to make it out there, she had to consider her own needs ahead of others.

Life as a runaway for this puppy must have been scary. When there were thunderstorms around our house, she would practically claw her way out of the area she was in to try to hide from them. One can only imagine what it must have been like for a little defenseless puppy outside in the elements amidst the Texas winds and storms. At nighttime when she would get ready to sleep, she would burrow under a blanket wrapped up and snuggled from head to toe. This burrowing behavior was apparently one of the ways that she had learned to protect herself.

Out in the weather, did she wonder if she had made a mistake by leaving that first house? I wonder what she considered to be better—her original home or the streets. Who knows what might have happened to lead her to choose vagrancy over shelter? This invites curiosity about what that first environment might have been like for her and what might have been going on in her mind. I imagined what her thoughts might have been like. *I'm gonna get out of this crazy place! The humans around here must be completely insane! I'm going to find myself a better place to live. Anything is better than this!*

One could assume that a stray would likely have a rejection complex. Low self-esteem and an expectation to be treated like an outcast would make sense. But not with *this* dog—not *this* girl. Once settled with us here in her new home, I brought out some treats. I gave one to Mack, and then as my eyes turned toward her, she was sitting there, perked, expectant, mouth slightly opened, with her soft brown almond-shaped smiling eyes looking up at me. She had hopeful eyes that seemed to say, "And now it's my turn" or "Where's mine?" She had absolutely no doubt whatsoever that she was going to be included and treated with the same dignity as Mack, who had already established his status as a member of this family. The message exuding from her little heart was a complete expectation of being welcomed and included. She did not question for one minute her standing in this new family or whether she would be wanted.

I was moved by her attitude. Her circumstances might have taught her to expect neglect, resistance, and exclusion. Likely, she had experienced a life of having to fight for resources, hoard, scrape together, and outwit other predators for her own sustenance. However, on this day, there was no apologetic shame in her demeanor at all. When opportunity presented itself, she showed no self-effacing attitude of "I don't deserve it. I'm an outsider, an inconvenience—just leave me the crumbs." No, regardless of whatever she had gone through in her survival, her life stance was, "Where's mine? I am equal, too."

She had not gone through psychoanalysis or cognitive therapy to learn to believe in her own dignity and worth. She had not taken an assertiveness training course or read a textbook on social skills, yet her expectation influenced me. Even though I had already planned to give her a snack just like Mack's, I found her attitude impressive.

The environment from which she had escaped presents a mystery. Was that an angry house? Was the owner abusive? Or were there just too many other sibling pups with whom to compete? From that previous environment and subsequently life on the streets, she did not let trauma hold her back—not even for one minute.

One might say that she hit the jackpot in her search for a new home to adopt. Yes, as I said, I think she picked us. Through the years I raised her, she received the same care as Mack. This included grooming, dog treats, great fluffy dog beds, medical care, and even doggy acupuncture and chiropractic work, as well as a doggy heart electrocardiogram test and heart murmur medication (as they both developed heart murmurs at some point). It's almost as if early in her life, she had made a decision. Her decision was, *"(When I'm finally big enough) I am going to get out of this place and find myself a home that will care for me, love me, and treat me well. I will find a place where I am wanted and included."* So she did.

Myndie was unforeseen and unexpected. She was chosen as the second pet—the dog for my dog. Nevertheless, she never seemed to think of herself as second. She wormed her way into my heart, the full impact of which I didn't realize until after she was gone. She was spunky and loudly expressive in her zest for life and activity, and though small in size, she was larger than life. When she was about to be given a treat or an outing, she would express joy with her whole body, jumping up and down, her tail wagging enthusiastically, and her exuberant eyes smiling.

* * *

The Power That Is in Your Attitude

Did you know that your attitude has the potential to reshape your outcome? Do you approach unknown circumstances with bright expectant eyes and an openness of heart? Even your most subtle mannerisms, posture, gestures, responses, vocal tone, facial expressions, and other nonverbal cues can deliver a transformative impact to a situation. You consciously or unconsciously communicate information to others. You are either inviting them to accept you or to reject you. You also signal to them whether to trust you, take you seriously, or discount you. Your attitude is reflected in your demeanor and the signals you communicate to others regularly, even without a word.

While we do not have control over other people's decisions and some situations are rigid, you do possess the potential to create a positive pathway to a better, unexpected outcome in many cases. Here is an example:

Imagine two different people standing in front of you, needing an opportunity you hold in your power. One person averts eye contact, holds their head downward, and their tone trails off into obscurity. The other smiles, looks at you with bright, interested eyes, listens, and speaks clearly with optimism. Each is communicating with you nonverbally well beyond their stated words. The first one is discouraging further engagement, while the second one is inspiring hope. Which person would inspire assurance for you?

It is true that there are conditions that are inflexible and beyond our control. There are also situations which, in your own wisdom, you may choose to avoid. It is important to recognize, however, that you do have a lot of power in your attitude and the expectations that you exude to others around you.

How to Make It Happen

For that job interview, learn about the company in advance and also focus on the aspects of the work that are interesting to you. Expect yourself to be a good candidate for that opportunity. If you are not yet a good candidate, become one. If you need more training in an area, pursue it. Equip yourself to be the best candidate that you can be. Reflect this positive attitude and genuine interest in your demeanor.

Over the years, I have been hired for positions in which I knew that I did not have stellar training nor experience, yet I communicated an attitude of willingness to learn and to bring a healthy work ethic to the position. I got hired in at least two positions simply because I continued to show interest by checking back for new openings after an initial rejection. Having been an employee, a business owner, and a manager in a large corporation, I can say that a person who is sincere, ethical, kind, and genuinely willing to grow into a work role can be preferable to an experienced genius who lacks the qualities of sincerity and character.

Your nonverbal gestures and attitude can impact your relationships either positively or negatively. Interpersonal dynamics can be steered into constructive outcomes with just the slightest adjustment of tone, softening of voice, or gentle smile. Do not be afraid to apologize and also give grace to others for their mistakes. Remember, relationships require work and sincerity just like a career does.

If you are willing to be a good partner, employee, friend, etc., and you downplay yourself or become lazy in your actions, you are simply denying that other person the opportunity to be blessed by all the good that you can bring to them. Begin to acknowledge the value that you bring to the table, and then you can communicate this authentically.

See Yourself the Way You Want Others to See You

Never consider yourself to be an afterthought, insignificant, or unwanted. I was the third-born child in a family only planning for two kids, yet I was never called an accident. If you were conceived unexpectedly, you were not an accident! You were—and *are*—a surprise and *ABSOLUTELY MEANT TO BE*. No matter HOW you came into the world, you were absolutely <u>*planned, wanted, and meant to be here*</u>. The fact that you were born means that YOU are supposed to be here and that someone, if not your parents, someone *higher* than your parents intended for you to be here. You were put here on this Earth for a good reason. Do not let anyone make you doubt that for one minute. You have your own unique purpose, and even if you do not know what that is just yet, you can discover it. Keep trying out your areas of interest and talent, and you will discover abilities that you did not know existed.

In April 2018, Amy Schumer starred in the movie *I Feel Pretty*.[1] She played the role of Renee Bennett, who struggled with low self-esteem and body-shame because she compared herself to the glamorous models in her career in the cosmetic industry. One day in her aerobic spin class, she worked out so intensely that she fell off her stationary bike and hit her head. When she came back into consciousness, she suddenly saw herself in the mirror as physically beautiful and flawless.

This transformed the entire manner in which Renee approached the world. Because of her new self-perception, she expected to be accepted. Her whole new attitude was one of complete confidence and carefree inhibition. No longer worried about the rejection of others, she was free to dive into the mission of her purpose. Now, no longer distracted with thoughts of what others might think about her, she plunged 100 percent of her energy and her full focus

---

[1] Abby Kohn and Marc Silverstein (directors). *I Feel Pretty*. STX Entertainment. 2018.

into being the best at whatever task and assignment she found in front of her.

Renee struck up conversations with friendly strangers and people in her field with exuberance, completely expecting to be treated as an equal. She began engaging with them, focused on the assignment, and ignored their sometimes perplexed reactions until she won them over.

This may be just a movie, but there is substance to the genuine expectation that you send out to the world. In many situations, you can send out kindness, and you will receive kindness. Send out rejection or the expectation thereof, and you will be inviting that very same negative response you fear to come back to you.

You can experiment with this idea in small forms. Perhaps start with people you know and trust at first. Begin to expect a change in their treatment of you by modeling it first to them. If you want acceptance, you may try to give them a well-chosen compliment—something truthful. You may want to ask a potential colleague or manager for a career opportunity, then follow it up with your entire body aligned with your expectation for your request to be given serious consideration.

Give Yourself Permission

Remember Myndie with her cheerful little bright-eyed smile that I could not refuse? This all starts with you deciding to become your own best friend, telling yourself that it is *absolutely* okay for you to be wanted and included. Myndie possibly did not encounter this type of treatment at her first house, so she searched until she found an environment that would welcome her and love her.

Give yourself permission to seek the training that you need for that career of your dreams. Continue to seek out the kind of friends who will love and support you. Begin to speak lovingly to yourself in your thought-life and align your body, posture, and behavior with this new attitude toward yourself.

When you make an error, be constructive with yourself rather than punitive. Be honest and realistic, combined with love and acceptance for your value. You are more than what others may think of you. Before they can begin to see your value, you must first allow yourself to see the treasure that is you.

Chapter Four

Embrace Joy and Play

When Mack and Myndie were both young, they would wrestle all through the house. It was never a dull moment. Early on, they learned a very important word they associated with their favorite activity—"the walk." Regularly, I would take them on a walk around the neighborhood, and it was fascinating to watch how Myndie would relish this activity. Side by side on their leashes, she would scamper and turn to look at Mack with her long skinny tongue hanging halfway out of her open mouth as if to say, "Isn't this fun?" She was relational and wanted to share her joy with her new companion, Mack. I was impressed by how she savored and enjoyed every playful moment.

Throughout her life, she never hesitated to expect good things to come to her and to be included in available opportunities. I couldn't even put on my exercise shoes without her beginning to rise up and start jumping around, animated and expecting to do the walk.

Myndie would remember fondly certain words associated with each experience that had become positive for her. "The walk," "green-green for the nite nite," (their bedtime treat), and even a phrase labeled for medical treatment when she was older. As one of these words or phrases was spoken, she would become energized and celebrate it with her whole body, jumping up and down (not as high now that she was becoming older) but her tail still wagging in full swing nevertheless and that broad smile.

When Myndie was about ten years old, something happened to the spinal column in her neck. It became swollen and inflamed. She could not move her head, and it was clear that she was in a lot of pain. Off to the emergency vet we went. They x-rayed her and ran other tests, but could only provide temporary relief for the pain. I knew of a nearby veterinarian/chiropractor/acupuncturist, so I made an appointment.

At her first appointment, she stood on the table, legs stiff, body frozen with trepidation as the vet applied needles in strategic places on her back, neck, and the meridians in her limbs. As she stood there, afraid to move, the perplexed look in her eyes seemed to ask, *"What's happening?"* I was encouraging her that this would help her by telling her words like "You'll feel better," a phrase with which she also became familiar with during her healing process. Each visit helped, and she eventually became completely healed. This doctor and only this doctor was associated with the words, "Let's go to the doctor." Every time I used that phrase when it was time for another acupuncture appointment, her whole body would become animated with joy. She would begin to jump up and down, tail wagging, panting with excitement, and that skinny tongue hanging out of her full, mouth-opened smile as she scampered toward the garage door. How in the world would a little being get so excited about getting poked with needles?

* * *

Do you let yourself play? Do you allow yourself to relish *your* joy? Can you feel excitement about an upcoming plan to play? Do you let yourself fully feel each of the blissful moments of fun, wonder, or glee when engaged in play? On the other hand, were you taught to think of play as a waste of time?

Some of us do not even allow ourselves to have this important activity known as downtime, fun, or play anywhere in our schedules. Furthermore, when we do schedule a fun event, sometimes we may hijack it from ourselves even while in the experience. We may rob ourselves of that exciting anticipation by worrying about whether things will go well. Then, while in the moment, we might further rob ourselves of full enjoyment of each moment if we are caught up in whether we served the right appetizers, wore the right clothes, or said the right words.

Do you sometimes make a plan to play, yet complicate it with so much pressure or high expectation that you turn the activity into yet another form of work? We can learn to keep our life in balance with work, rest, and play.

What is Play?

I define play as any healthy activity that brings you joy. For one person, it may be playing or watching sports. For another, it may be doing a creative project or watching a movie. Play is something you need to recharge your energy so that you can rest better and work more effectively. For many people, some forms of work are play for them because, to them, that particular form of work feels enjoyable.

The important question is two-fold:

1. Do you give yourself enough playtime?
2. Are you living in the moment when you *do* play?

This is what was so memorable to me about Myndie. She would become exuberant even at the anticipation of the upcoming playful event. Once she heard one of those words she recognized, before it even happened, she would experience that excitement with her whole body. And, while it was happening, she would enjoy every moment of it all the way through. During any play activity, you could see that she was relishing each moment, one by one, fully present. There was no distraction from future worries nor past regrets.

Not only do we need to give ourselves permission to take time for pleasant activities, but we also need to be fully present when we are in each of those moments. I learned this a long time ago, and it has helped me to be a productive human being. I currently work more than sixty-five hours per week. I have set play and rest as high in my priorities and follow them faithfully.

I have designated every Friday, during the day, as "SPA Day." Now, this does not mean that I go to expensive spas and spend oodles of money. I call it SPA to remind myself to relish whatever the needed play (and rest) activities are for that day. While on Sundays I consistently give myself the day off to rest, on Fridays I consider what I need the most to restore my emotional balance. If I want comic relief, I seek out a funny movie. If I feel the need for pampering, I may schedule a SPA activity or just get a foot massage. On many days, I have just simply piled up with the TV and my dogs, a SPA activity I call "naps with dogs."

Your playtime can be simple, inexpensive, and even brief. Sometimes in the middle of a workday, having lunch with a friend or taking a nice walk can rejuvenate and replenish you emotionally for the remainder of the workday. I like to call each of these brief perks a "Sprinkle of SPA."

Appreciate even the smallest and simplest perks that come your way—especially the unexpected ones. Myndie expressed joy, anticipation, and appreciation for every small blessing offered to her—a snack, a walk, and even acupuncture.

Play takes on several forms and is in the eye of the beholder. Some forms of work constitute play. Your career may have several enjoyable aspects that can fulfill your emotional need for an uplift. Constructive and restorative activity that you enjoy, such as sports, going to the gym, watching a movie, listening to comedy, doing a creative project, reading, or even sitting quietly to take in nature, can all qualify as play. Intersperse play into your life in both large and small quantities. Take a weeklong vacation whenever you can. Take a day off once in a while when you need it.

Why Play?

Play brings joy. It can reduce stress and renew your attitude. Both rest and play can refresh your energy and restore your soul.

At present, I work in several roles, both in private practice and in employment as a unit manager in behavioral health. This creates a very long workweek and long workdays. This is why I make sure to give myself a SPA Day of both rest and play every Friday during the first half of the day and sometimes the full day. I also distribute these perks throughout the week as well.

While play recharges your energy and is good for your mental health, it can also recharge your relationships with others. A powerful strategy for helping couples in marital therapy is to just get them to go out on dates. This has been an approach for marital therapy for decades. Often, given no other deep-seated psychological issues, this alone can renew the relationship.

Play is a way that people bond. I have found this to be true in my work with couples. Think about how couples often get together in the first place. They usually go out and do things that are fun. They spend time getting to know each other through various activities and, one day, tie the knot.

What happens with many couples once they cross the threshold? Work. Now, I am not saying that work is negative. *Au contraire*, I love work. Here, however, the marriage script or the partner script steps in. The fun times often begin to decrease and become overshadowed by work roles. Who is supposed to take out the trash? Who is supposed to cook or clean? How about this answer? Both, either, or neither.

Many couples become so obsessed with how to do this marriage thing right that they destroy it. Absorption in who is supposed to do what "now that we are together" can zap the romance and have you forgetting the reason you got together in the first place.

It is important to give play a place in several areas of your life. Even some of those work chores can be intermingled with fun. Play your favorite music while cleaning—play it loudly and dance with the vacuum cleaner or mop. As a couple, you can turn household chores into creative fun that comes alive with play.

Here's the Deal

We can all take a chapter from Myndie's playbook. Take time to play and savor each experience to the fullest. Its effect can linger like a pleasant memory to help carry you through some of those dry spells that might be ahead. Don't let yourself miss out on the laughter, the wonder, and the glee.

Remember, you cannot fully experience the regenerative benefit of play if you do not savor each moment and appreciate the small surprises. You can find something amusing or interesting even with imperfection. Don't rob yourself of your much-needed rejuvenation by expecting things to be perfect. If the line is long, if you encounter traffic, or the meal is not to your ideal expectation, focus on what parts of the event have been positive.

Keep your life in balance. Too much play and too much work can bring you out of balance. You need a fairly even distribution of all three: work, rest, *and* play.

Lastly, don't analyze your ice cream. Just enjoy it!

Chapter Five

Don't Ever Think You Are Too Small to Have a Big Voice

One day at a veterinarian's office, when my son and I were paying for the services, there was the tiniest little kitten behind the counter, sitting at the bottom of a large box and looking up at us. She was the last one left from a litter of cats that had been abandoned in an alley. She sat there just waiting for someone to claim her. There she was… a grey and white tabby with innocent eyes looking up at us. Without hesitation, we took her home.

She looked just like a cat my family had during my childhood we called Kitty Tom. It was difficult to come up with a name that would exactly fit her, so we just called her Kitty. This quiet, unassuming feline lived for twenty-one years, only having a health issue during her last year of life.

She had a placid nature and got along well with the other pets we brought into the house throughout the years, including our Rottweiler. She never demanded attention and only meowed when she was very hungry. Kitty was the type of cat who minded her own business and did not disrupt the routine. She remained peaceful and quiet regardless of events around her.

Years ago, after this cat had become older, I had taken an elderly woman, Kay, under my wing who had been a neighbor for the past twenty years. Her family situation had erupted into chaos. One thing led to another, when all at once, just before her 87th birthday, she was losing both her home and her relationships with all of her family members.

This was a very heart-wrenching situation for her as well as her family. They were all becoming estranged from each other. For decades, she had lived in the home with them, helping to raise the grandchildren who were now grown.

Years before, I would sometimes go over there when my son played with her grandchildren, and I would see her working in the kitchen. It seemed that she had sacrificed everything for them and had hoped to be able to live with them in that home for the rest of her life. This was no longer going to be the case. The events that ensued clutched my heart and, honestly, I believed that God wanted me to help her.

I raised money for her, helped to connect her to professional resources, and helped her find a new place to live. Her family had stopped talking to her during and after an unfortunate civil court process. When the dust had settled, she finally got up the courage to call her closest one, her granddaughter. Both reunited with tears and a warmth that rekindled as if nothing had ever happened. I was so happy about this reunion that I felt a big sigh of relief from my soul. That evening, I thought maybe I could finally relax and get the long-awaited rest that I had not had for months. At least the one with whom she was closest had come back into her life.

Now, deep sleep has rarely ever been a challenge for me. Some people are light sleepers, but not me. A story was told about my sister and I sleeping through a robbery. Yes, you are reading this correctly—a robbery. When we were young—I was very little—we shared a bedroom, and apparently a thief broke into our house. The noise of his break-in was, in fact, right by our ears. As he tried to climb through our bedroom window, he was also said to have knocked over several things on the nightstand right beside our beds. I didn't know. I was soundly asleep and so was my sister.

How did we find out? Our next-door neighbor heard him from far across her lawn, breaking into our room! When my neighbor called my parents, the guy was scared away and left us alone, unharmed. Everything turned out okay, thank Heavens.

Yes, I'm a deep sleeper. So that night, after I felt such relief that my elderly friend had just reunited with her granddaughter, I went into a deeper sleep than I had had in a long time. My comfortable bed had a chair close to it that no one ever used. It was positioned near the foot of my bed mainly just for decoration. Kitty usually slept on the floor. My cell phone stayed on with the charger intact, thinking that if anyone needed to contact me, they could. Deep into the covers I went, finally, for a long-awaited oasis of blissful rest. I was out.

Piercing through the wee hours of the morning, suddenly breaking through into my abyss of a deep, blissful coma, a shrill, relentless noise began to loudly interject itself into my oblivion. Never, ever had I heard this cat make such a screeching sound… and she was doing it repetitively. Kitty was sitting up on that chair at the foot of my bed, perched toward me, emitting the loudest shrieks and cries, urgently meowing over and over again.

I roused myself back into the land of the living and checked on her. She had no evidence of pain or injury. Everything in the house was normal. Then I looked at my cell phone and found that all through the night, my elderly friend, Kay, had been calling me, repeatedly, hour after hour, leaving several voice messages saying that she was feeling very sick and needed me to come. She was not in a state to drive herself to a place for medical assistance. I had not heard my phone even though it was not on silent mode. It was completely out of character for my friend to call like that. I called her back immediately and then called 911, and an ambulance was dispatched to her apartment. I met them at her apartment and then followed them to the ER.

Why did my cat meow like this on that one particular night? What led Kitty to persist? It was only her repeated shrills that finally broke through my deep sleep—nothing else. She had never behaved that way before nor since. Even during her last year of life, she quietly dealt with her medical discomfort without any attempt to wake me or get my attention during the night. This was the only time in her life that she had ever let out such a desperate meow. Because of that tiny little being bellowing out a persistent loud cry, I was able to help my friend.

* * *

What happened that day, I believe, was divine intervention. What are the odds that the cat would meow like that, having no discomfort and never having done that before? There is no way that Kitty knew why my phone kept ringing, nor what was on my voicemail. This was not an accident. I personally believe that God can speak through and work through even the smallest of us.

What About You?

Have there been times when you believed that your voice was too small or that you might not be important enough to play a role in something meaningful or important? Have you ever felt a strong urge to speak up but stopped yourself? Did you tell yourself things like, "Maybe I am wrong. I'm not as smart as them. Maybe they will figure it out. Maybe they already have the answer?"

Sometimes, if you believe that your idea may be needed or helpful, you can offer others the opportunity to hear it. There is a tactful way in which to do this. To avoid offering unsolicited advice, which some people may either welcome or resent, you can first ask for an opening to share. For example, you can say something like, "I have some thoughts on that" or "I have an idea." Then you can add "Would you like to hear?" or "Can I share it?" What can happen next is that they say "Okay," giving you permission to share your thoughts, and you have not given intrusive, unwanted information. If they say "No," you have offered and been thoughtful in your intention to help them, even if you do not get to share your wisdom. Their refusal to hear your idea does not mean that it was a bad one. You can then politely respect their refusal and interpret it as a refusal of only your idea and not a rejection of you personally. If you give no further advice, they may very well have missed out on wisdom that you had available for them, which is their loss, not yours.

Times to Speak Up

There may be times to speak up to save a life or take a firm stand when there is no permission given or it is even resisted. Speaking up in these instances may not allow time for questions. Do not be afraid to take a stand when you need to do so for the welfare of someone—including yourself. If someone gets upset with you, this may be more about what is going on with *them* than with you, especially if it is for their or your own welfare. Don't ever think you are too small to have a big voice or for your efforts to have relevance.

During my high school years, on a dark night, I was the passenger in the front seat of my friend's car. We were going about 60 or 70 mph and had just passed a car on the single-lane highway. We were still in the oncoming lane of traffic but had cleared the car behind us enough to move back over into our own lane. For some reason, my friend stayed frozen at the steering wheel, not moving back into our lane, as I saw the headlights of an oncoming car heading toward us. My friend, with hands frozen on the steering wheel, said in a slow, paralyzed voice, "Joan . . . . we're going to have a wreck."

Now, back then, I was shy and submissive, never resisting others' choices. I was very passive and easily bossed around. So, what I did next was uncharacteristic of me. Without a word, I just quietly reached over to the steering wheel and moved our car back into our own lane, averting a serious collision. The oncoming car passed by on the other side uneventfully. My friend then began to scream, loudly lecturing me and repeatedly saying, "Don't *EVER* grab the steering wheel! Don't *EVER* grab the wheel!" I did not argue back but just stayed silent.

It was not my nature to argue or disagree with my peers. However, if I had not crossed the boundary that day, stepped outside my own timidity by reaching over to my friend's side of the car, taken the steering wheel, and guided us back to our side of the road, I probably would not be here today writing this book to you. Sometimes there are times to speak up or take a stand, even if people get angry.

You Have a Voice and a Purpose

Do you ever doubt your potential to do something beyond your current status quo? Did someone ever dash your dreams? Did an authority over you tell you that you cannot, you are not good enough, you will never be able to, or that you will not amount to anything? Let me ask you this question. Who made them God? Who gave them that authority? The authority to block your potential? No one. I am 100 percent confident that the fact that you are here on this Earth—that you exist—means that you are here for a reason and meant for a good purpose. You have a worthwhile calling, no matter what anyone says and no matter what has already gone wrong.

It is my firm belief that the creator of the universe has put you here with a positive intention, no matter what your DNA, family history, lineage, or generational curse tries to speak otherwise. They are wrong. God is right. It is just that plain and simple. God has the authority over all of them, and He has a positive plan for your life.

Therefore, never question your ability to contribute something good to your circumstances. No matter how small you are, you can learn to accomplish great things with a little faith, open-mindedness to explore your gifts, proper training, and patience with yourself. You may be young and have some interests that you have yet to explore. On the other hand, you may have already lived through a long career, and it may be time to reach back into the archives, resurrect, and dust off that buried dream that got lost under that pile of obligations where you sacrificed for those you love. I believe that it is never too late to do something great.

Putting Your Voice into Action

How do you do this? Look at areas for which you have a passion to learn, grow, or help others. Explore some of those avenues. You can read about them and sometimes even volunteer in those environments. If it is an area of talent development, sign up for a class. This can show you whether or not you will truly want to pursue that aspiration. If you cannot afford tuition, some professions may not require traditional training. There may be some resources online or opportunities for on-the-job training. There are also many areas of work that need assistants or other employees or volunteers at various levels of training. Even if you are not the top dog, you could possibly become part of a team participating with others in something greater than yourself alone.

Spend even just a few minutes daily if you can, working on that talent or studying that vocation. The consistent dedication of even your tiniest, persistent effort invested over time can result in an amazing outcome.

You may want to finally start that college degree or vocational training program that had deterred you because of the months or years it may take to complete. What if by the time you finish the training, you are X number of years old? You will likely get that old anyway; why not get there with a degree under your belt as well? You then have that degree or that certificate of training and a license to work in the field in which you had dreamt.

Your Dream Awaits

Never second-guess or doubt your potential to do something important. I truly believe that miracles often come in small packages and from the least expected places. What an amazing and pleasant surprise it is when that happens. It is never too late, and you are never too powerless to pursue many of your dreams and ambitions. Allow yourself to explore options, pursue the training of your passions, and reach through the doors of your dreams. If one door is closed, reach for another one. It is often that our areas of interest and passion may very well be indicators of our destiny—of our calling.

Divine intervention can come in a boundless array of forms. I believe that when your heart or your intention is right, the creator of the universe can do boundless things through you. Commit to remaining open to learning and growing. Listen to wise teachers and read spiritual scripture for guidance as well. When the passions of your heart align with reality and morality, that is a good start.

Sometimes it takes something outside the norm to get our attention, just like the incident with my cat, Kitty, that day. I would definitely call that a divine interruption. Allow yourself to be interrupted on occasion. It might just point you to something important in which you are needed. Don't be afraid to step into it.

Chapter Six

Know Your Power

Years ago, we had a Rottweiler named Charlie. She was actually a teddy bear inside, but no one knew it by looking at her. She grew up to weigh ninety-five pounds. Every time I took her walking, everyone would cross over to the opposite side of the street whether they were walking alone or with their pet. I believed that they were afraid of her just because of her appearance.

Rottweilers have often been misunderstood as potentially aggressive. They certainly can be powerful and strong. Not this dog. She was very gentle and loving. Her best friend in our house was Kitty, our cat. I would watch them together in the kitchen. Charlie would be lying on the floor and Kitty would be grooming the top of her head with nurturing cat kisses. They would often relax together and just hang out all day long. Charlie was quiet and very sweet-natured.

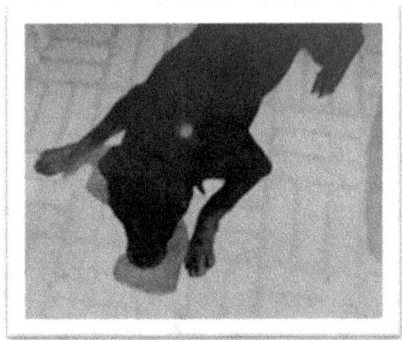

With a personality like Gentle Ben, she had no idea how she looked to others. They could only see her outward appearance and could not read her spirit inside. As a single mom, I did enjoy the terrified look in the eyes of strange men outside my front door when she would walk up to stand beside me inside the foyer to see what they wanted.

She had no idea during walks why passersby would cross on to the opposite side of the road. She had no inkling of how ominous she appeared to others. I think she might have read their reactions as rejection. If not for Kitty being her best friend, I think she would have been very lonely.

* * *

Misinterpretation of First Impressions

Do people ever misread you? Do you sometimes assume their reactions to you as indicative of rejection? They may just be misreading you by only seeing the outer package. Sometimes they may need an opportunity to have more information if they are willing to be open. It can be worth the time to see if they are just misreading you, and then give them a little time to know the good that exists within you.

We cannot force someone to be willing to look deeper and get to know us. We can offer them the opportunity by extending kindness to them, yet the rest is up to them. Some people have more rigid social barriers than others, and that is their right. Everyone gets to choose their own boundaries, and some people prefer to limit their social circle. This is likely more about them than about you and not necessarily an indicator of anything being wrong with either one of you. If someone is not willing to reciprocate a friendship, be patient in your search for someone who is.

I wonder how many neighbors missed out on getting to know Charlie's sweet personality. I wonder if she felt lonely because of this, but it is possible that she did not. She seemed to know that she was loved and was perhaps content and secure within herself.

First, See the Good Within Yourself

Whether or not someone is willing to see the good within you, it is first important for you to recognize it in yourself. No one can see you in a positive light until you begin to see the good that exists within you first.

It was not until I was in my mid-twenties that I learned that it is okay to recognize the value that resides within yourself. I was taught to be very humble, and believe me, I was good at it! If you do not know what is inside your own package, you will not know the treasure that you have to offer the world. For anything good to be delivered from within you, first there must be knowledge—knowledge of your potential. Therefore, the first step in you becoming that wonderful blessing to the world (that you are meant to be) is for you to recognize the positive ingredients you have to offer. Believe me, you do have positive things inside you to offer, no matter who has told you otherwise.

How to Discover Your Assets Within

One way to discover your potential within is to ask yourself the following questions:

- What are your passions, interests, and hopes?

- Do you feel an interest in helping people in a certain way?
- Are you driven to work with numbers or computers?
- Do you like to work with your hands, or do you prefer to work with ideas?
- Are you drawn to work with people?
- What do you find intriguing?

You may have gifts inside you that have not yet been awakened. Take time to explore them. Don't be afraid to try an avenue, and if it doesn't work out, try a different one.

Take a moment and picture yourself engaged in an area that interests you. Allow yourself to imagine and envision yourself in that role. Every person born has at least one talent and often more. You must first see it on the horizon of your future. Then you can pursue the knowledge and training necessary to achieve it. Don't worry about how long it takes. If it is a profession that embraces your passion and purpose, you are likely to enjoy the adventure along the way.

What is True Power?

There are different types of power and strength. True power is not necessarily loud or aggressive. Sometimes strength comes in quiet gentleness. I am sure that if Charlie wanted to, she could overpower a grown man and inflict certain harm, but she never needed to use her strength in that manner. She just stood there being herself, with her broad head and muscular body—no one needed to look any further.

Power is best shown in counterintuitive ways. It takes more strength to restrain aggression than to brazenly display it. When someone really possesses power, it is not likely to be loud or flamboyant. They exude the quiet confidence in their knowledge or talent for which they have worked hard, with no need to prove anything to anyone. On our walks, Charlie just quietly let her neighbors cross on over to the other side of the street without protest.

The most influential power can be manifested through the gentleness of compassion, the loyalty of caring, and the sacrifice of commitment. It takes a bigger person to restrain an impulse, hold back from retaliating to a cheap shot, or refrain from getting to have the last word in an argument.

Many years ago, I was a musical soloist in a Christian band. We were young adults who would travel together to do concerts on weekends. One of our musicians (first name, Mike), happened to also be a bodybuilder. You could tell by just looking at him that he was likely to be extremely strong. During a summer rehearsal, I remember thinking that his thighs seemed as large as tree trunks. He was always soft-spoken and kind, like a big Gentle Ben, too. You could say that he was like a Rottweiler version of a person, strong and clearly able to outwrestle anyone who might dare to try.

In one of our meetings, we were discussing some of our different doctrines and beliefs. After a few of us had gone around the table sharing thoughts, two members of the band got into a heated disagreement. It did not involve any name-calling or bad language but it did become very vocal and loud between the two. I had never seen this happen in our group before, so I just sat there stunned in silence. I think everyone was dumbfounded and speechless.

The tirade between the two continued on for a few more moments without intervention. Suddenly, the normally quiet, massively strong bodybuilder in our group burst into tears. Without raising his voice even one decibel, this big man expressed to all of us in sadness and fervor that he hates strife. As he wiped the tears from his face, the whole room immediately fell into a hushed silence. He then said, "I love you like a brother" (Personal communication, September 28, 2025). In an instant, the argument was completely shut down. To this day, I don't even remember what its topic had been. In one gentle, yet powerful, authentic response, he had brought chaos to a screeching halt. I will never forget that moment.

True Power

True power and strength come from a true heart. This strong musician did not have to raise his voice, display a physical outburst, or show one ounce of aggression. In this example, phenomenal power was displayed through a single act of sincerity and tenderness. While there is nothing wrong with physical strength displayed when needed, sincere tenderness can at times prove to be more powerful than the loud noise of an escalating argument. In one single moment, this gentle giant of a musician abruptly brought the chaos to a crashing halt.

It takes a lot more strength to keep the peace than to win an argument. You may be able to recall times when a completely unexpected response, such as a soft voice or an understanding response, became a complete game changer, rather than the anticipated matched hostility. Think of examples when someone may have easily reacted with hate when revenge seemed justified, yet they didn't. An unexpected, calm response can have the element of surprise and can sometimes leave the instigator challenged, grasping for what to do next. For example, if someone is yelling at you, while still showing them respect, you can choose to give a soft-tone response with words that acknowledge their need in some way. This can sometimes shut down the whole debacle.

This is not a message about being passive or letting others walk on you. It is an example for those times when it is wise to take the higher ground. When people are upset, they need (or at least perceive that they need) something. When things are not working for them, the natural tendency is to display anger. The best and most succinct definition of anger that I have ever heard is that it is energy designed to repair. And when you look beneath anger, you can find a hidden level of need, fear, hurt, or other sensitive core emotion.

Times to Step in and Times to Step Back

Clearly, there are some situations that are not wise or safe to go into. If the person is physically aggressive or dangerous, protect yourself and get away from them. Analyze them later… from a distance. It may be fruitless to attempt to stick around and try to empathize or reason with them if they are flagrantly psychotic, under the influence of substances, or in need of medical attention. This may not be the time to try to reason with them.

These are cases when a person cannot understand reason, even if you do everything by the book. At these times, professional help may be necessary, and you are helping them the most by calling 911.

There are times to speak up and times to wait. Experience can help you develop this skill of discernment. Sometimes the other person is just not willing to listen, and other times it could even be unsafe to engage with them. During these incidents, remind yourself that you did the best that you could.

A Special Form of Power

If they are not dangerous, you may have a few more options. Generally, beneath a raving lunatic is usually a very scared child at heart. This is not to simplify all the psychological philosophies throughout history nor to excuse other people's misbehavior. It is a perspective that can give you insight. It may be that our only task is to quietly step back and understand without trying to rescue, lecture, or fix them.

Sometimes, using your imagination to consider the underlying need inside that person may soften the dynamics. Allowing yourself to consider the possible need or feeling underneath their anger can give you the upper hand in managing the situation. This is different from trying to read their minds, which none of us can do and may also come across as a bit intrusive to them anyway. As long as they are still able to use reason, you might ask them, "What do you need right now?" "What can I do to help?" This is a powerful method that involves a gentle willingness to approach the situation with neutral curiosity and acceptance rather than judgment.

This perspective can give you strength. It gives you an awareness that their actions may be about something already going on with them, not you. Know that it is not your job to counsel them about whatever is going on beneath the surface but that of a professional. Your role can be to give them emotional support or understanding and help them find the appropriate professional intervention.

Willingness to understand is a powerful gift called empathy. It is not the same thing as sympathy. Sympathy involves feeling sorry for the person and can feel demeaning or condescending to them. Empathy is a supportive and powerful level of compassion. It can help the person to feel seen or understood. There is something profound about the feeling that someone is willing to see things through your eyes even when they disagree—that can soothe the soul.

Chapter Seven

Don't Be So Mesmerized by the Prize That You Fall for Hidden Sneaky Lies

As the story goes, one day, my brother-in-law brought home a sweet little puppy he found. He was a golden retriever/collie mix whose energy knew no bounds. They decided to name him Champ, which was very fitting because every day he would fill their lives with fun and enthusiasm. My sister and brother-in-law enjoyed watching Champ run the gamut of their large backyard and play fetch.

Champ was always a winner. As a one-year-old, he was still a bundle of energy, running eagerly to catch the ball, playing tug of war with the rope, obliterating the squeaker, or romping over the biggest mound he could find in their yard. Day after day, he was an energetic ball of entertainment for them, and life was perfect in their great backyard.

Now, as much as my brother-in-law loved that dog, he also loved to do yard work, and he was quite the perfectionist. The landscapes of every home in which they lived were immaculate, and it was all due to his handiwork. *What a great idea it would be,* he thought one day, *to plant a layer of new, rich fresh grass over that whole backyard.* So, he went to the garden store and bought lots of pallets of fresh sod.

Now, when I say he was a perfectionist, I am not kidding. He carefully laid out all the pallets and meticulously cut them into identical strips. Then he got down on his hands and knees, focusing on each small section of the yard in front of him, one at a time. He carefully planted one piece of sod, perfectly placed it, then inched forward to plant the next, then the next, never veering from side to side nor looking anywhere else. He exclusively focused on each section in front of him, expecting to just sit back at the end with a glow of pride over his hard-earned creation.

While he was methodically creating what he planned to be the perfect lawn, Champ had other ideas. This dog had a whole different interpretation of what was going on. In Champ's mind, it might have gone something like this: *Wow! My person is starting a whole new game!! What is this cool new stuff? This is a new toy like I have never seen before! I think I have seen the game Leapfrog, but this one is different. He's laying a whole bunch of new toys down here just for me to follow behind him! What a great friend!* (Champ makes a big, broad dog smile.)

At each interval, Champ eagerly bit into the piece of sod in front of him (and behind my brother-in-law's back), shook it, and ravaged it in a frenzy of joyous glee. Doggie paws, dirt, and grass were flying everywhere! One by one, Champ followed in step behind him, grabbing the one that was just planted, digging it up, and wrestling it into oblivion. On and on they went around the whole yard until each piece of sod had been laid (and then obliterated). To Champ, *Oh! What fun is this new game! I really LIKE my person a lot!!*

Finally, my exhausted brother-in-law (Champ's adored person), slowly and stiffly raised from his kneeling position to admire the prize of his hard labor. He turned to see a very grateful and satisfied dog broadly smiling up at him, tail wagging. Champ was covered from head to toe with sod, standing in the middle of a landscape that looked like it had been hit by a cyclone. Every square inch of his beautiful creation had been turned upside down right behind him. No photo could capture the look on my brother-in-law's face at that moment. (*Best friend ever!!* thought Champ.)

This example is not merely about yard work or pets. There are also definitely times for us to keep our eye on the prize, not look back, nor give in to distractions around us. The Champ story here, however, symbolically represents some valuable lessons of a different kind that some of us may have had to learn the hard way.

That Sparkling Prize

Ever become taken in by that radiant gem in the jewelry case or that additional new car on the lot? You know that dazzling one-of-a-kind prize in front of you, taking over your entire attention span? Ever become seduced by that great sales pitch? You may be thinking that you can't live without it, but somehow you've managed to live without it just fine all your life up until this moment. To make things worse, the sales agent is telling you that you better act now or it will be gone. The cleverly trained salesperson knows exactly what to say.

Perhaps you leave the store, but you can't seem to get it out of your mind—you know, that awesome shiny thing with all its bells and whistles. Maybe you resist initially and go home thinking that you outwitted that financial snare, only to find that you can't seem to stop thinking about it. Everywhere you look, you see one just like it. Everyone seems to have one. It hijacks your focus, perhaps obstructing the blessings you already have around you. You aren't looking at those blessings for which you already spent your hard-earned money. You are only fixated on that new one that you don't have.

Perhaps this might be related to a relationship. If you are already in a good one, have you ever felt mesmerized by someone who seems prettier, more handsome, smarter, stronger, wealthier, more talented, more athletic, or more glamorous? Do all those positive traits of that loved one in your life seem to fade into the background now that you encounter this new, intriguing person?

The grass often *does* seem greener on the other side. Other people's spouses, partners, and family members often do seem to act nicer, but that is just on the outside. They may be acting that way because you (and other people) are watching. This tendency to behave a bit better in public is human nature. Furthermore, that new attraction may know just what to say or how to treat you—just like the salesperson.

Oh, the hidden surprises that can lurk behind that sparkly curtain once exposed! Eventually, that shiny gem fades and gets thrown into the jewelry box with all the other once-shimmering trinkets. The new car may not break down as fast as the previous one, but the insurance coverage that comes with it may be a whole new, unexpected adversary. The new partner, once secure in a new relationship with you, may reveal their own quirks that make your previous partner now seem like a nostalgic oasis. If this new relationship began from either one of you betraying a current partner, is it possible that they may one day betray you?

We learn in life that even people can sometimes prop themselves up to look like a "Champ." They can polish up and make themselves shiny just like that sparkling gem under the store lights, and promote to us a field of dreams. Once behind that sparkly curtain, however, we may find that we have embarked upon something we did not anticipate.

Now, I am not telling you to pass up nice things for yourself or avoid some of life's finer indulgences. Nor am I telling you to remain in any relationship that is not good for you. Sometimes change is necessary. I am also not encouraging you to have a distrustful attitude toward new opportunities, nor resist new adventures.

There are times to have a committed focus on your dreams. Do pursue your ambitions, but do not be so tunnel-visioned that you allow your hyperfocus to exclude other important areas in your life so that they do not become stolen from behind you.

Strength Under Pressure

What about that "friend" who tries to pressure you into doing something with which you are not comfortable? How about that person you've been dating who is trying to get you to do something that you do not want to do? If they are pressuring you into doing something that you have told them you are not ready for or have peace of mind about doing, then they may not be the best influence for you. Anyone who tries to pressure you into doing something that violates your conscience is thinking of themselves instead of you and is not really your friend.

Something We Can Learn from a Toddler

There is a powerful two-letter word that toddlers discover in their infinite wisdom and begin to use sometimes more freely than we may like at the time. It is the word "No." This is not a bad word, nor is it inherently disrespectful, although you may want to teach them to apply it with a respectful tone. This is our first application of boundary setting. Given that with maturity we learn how to flex on some of our "Nos" in getting along with others, a true friend (or a mature one) will not want you to compromise your own values just to give them what they want at the time. It is okay to wait when you do not feel peace in your heart and to say the word "No." You can also augment it into a phrase of "Not now."

Giving yourself time to pause for a moment can save you unwanted stress. The strategies below are to help you consider ways to use discernment and wise judgment so that a hypnotizing sparkle does not lead you into an obliterated jungle.

See Your Mistakes as a Springboard Into Growth

There are times when we do find our lives in shambles. I am 100 percent certain that if this is you, it is still not too late to recover. I have seen this truth over and over again in my counseling profession, enough to tell you that the fact that you are here means there is still hope for you and your future. No matter how far you have gone down the wrong road, it is not too late to turn around and get your life back on track, one piece at a time.

Our mistakes can actually be our greatest lessons. I would much rather learn from someone who really knows what it is like to walk through a mistake and learn from experience than someone who has never tasted regret. So, give yourself a big dose of mercy, forgiveness, and permission to overcome. What you have walked through may very well turn out to be the exact training ground for your next purpose and assignment in your life.

If you are young, it is great to learn these concepts as early as you can. If you are in an older age group, let's say "mature" (as I like to call it now that I am in that group!), it is never too late to learn. The following are some strategies that can save us all from being pulled into a mess. I address two important areas of our lives: financial and relational.

Wise Strategies

1. Think it through.

Before you take the plunge, give yourself plenty of time to think it through. Thinking it through gives you time to research and weigh other options.

Take the time to compare products at other stores and look for better prices. Also, give yourself time to listen to your gut. See if you feel a sense of peace. You may feel a twinge of doubt. If so, hold off.

One of my best career positions involved an additional role on a team for a renowned psychiatrist and author who was beginning to teach professional continuing education programs. One of the things that fascinated me was an assignment to take ample time to interview several different vendors and compare their prices and policy structures. We were tasked with the mission of waiting until we had examined each one and then strategically comparing them before deciding on the final choice. This tiny part of my role in that company made a big impression and stuck with me.

There were several lessons here:

a. Take your time to explore all available options.

b. Make them wait before you decide.

c. Compare and contrast to determine the most beneficial choice.

d. Don't let yourself be rushed in this decision process.

In the real world, there are very few cases in which you must "act now" in a purchase. Some exceptions exist, but I believe they are rare. Take your time to compare prices; check out other stores to see if that same (or even better) item is on sale somewhere else. You may be surprised by the options you discover. This can also apply to relationships. Take your time to make sure that this is the person for you before you take the plunge. There is more about this further on.

Just because someone says they have a product that will make you great, wonderful, smarter, prettier, stronger, or more handsome, do the research. Don't just take their word at face value. Examine what they say. Compare them with their competitors and read reviews. Make sure that you do not fall prey to someone who just wants to make a buck and doesn't really care about you.

How Long to Wait?

Sometimes we may not know if we are waiting too long for a decision. It is okay to give yourself a little time to think first and balance it with not waiting too long on a choice. I cannot tell you when to decide or what to decide, but I can tell you that actions made in haste may often lead to regrets.

If you give yourself a little time, you can weigh the options. Perhaps sleep on it or consult with someone. If it lines up with logical common sense, your moral conscience, and you feel peace in your spirit about the decision, this could indicate a positive direction.

2. Rein in your emotions for important decisions.

Sometimes we are so tempted to take the plunge. We may feel a strong emotional pull to give in to the sales rep or the attractive romantic lure. I have become a firm believer in the maxim that if it is meant for you, it will wait for you. This does not mean to wait forever on a decision or keep your fiancé or fiancée eternally waiting in the wings, but just give yourself a little time to let the emotions calm down.

Every important decision needs to have a logical foundation. Your decision needs to match up with your moral code, align with common sense, and sometimes incorporate how it may affect those around you. This does not mean sacrificing all your desires for others. Sometimes people can be manipulators (see further down). However, make sure that the choice you are considering includes in-depth thought and wisdom.

You Can Protect Your Resources

A speaker once presented a brilliant psychological question about money in an interview. They asked, "If money walked into your house one day and sat down in front of you, what would it say? What is the first thought that comes to your mind?" Back then, the first thought that came to my mind was, *I'm not going to be here long!*

Some people have a fear of money, goods, resources, and opportunities being stolen from them, so much so that they spend it way too fast, as if they will never get another opportunity. This is one example of emotional spending. Examine your emotions, thought processes, and actions, and you may be happy that you did.

The businessperson may very well care about your money more than your welfare. If the item is on sale, it may go on sale again later. Stores are designed to ramp up the glitz and sometimes pressure the buyer, but make them wait. Years ago, I had been told that a couple of exotic pants suits were going to go on sale, so I waited. On the day of the sale, the rep told me that one was on sale, but the other one (the one I had indicated I wanted) was not. So, without skipping a beat, I turned my back toward her and started going out of the store, calmly saying, "Then, I don't want it."

Immediately, she spoke up and said, "Wait." Then gave it to me for the sale price.

Also, don't fall for the "buy now and pay later" scheme. Young adults may receive the greatest number of credit card offers of all the populations in the United States. This may be one of the sneakiest maneuvers by some of our financial institutions. The fine print of credit card applications may reveal more than you can imagine. When you charge something that you are not able to completely pay off at the end of the month, the interest (interest-ing only for the bank's deep pockets!) can sneak up on you. Credit cards are okay for emergencies or building cash back benefits. Other than that, they can become a trap that hijacks your finances, and you are paying more to some fat financial entity than to yourself. People often become prey to this crafty web due to impulse buying and emotional spending.

Allow yourself time to wait before you jump. Take time to let your emotions quell so that you can apply sound thinking and decision-making in the process. After giving it deeper thought, you may discover better options that you would have missed by acting in haste. When we react too quickly to our emotions, it can often lead to disappointment.

3. Learn to tap into your intuition.

Your intuition is your God-given compass. It can guide you with internal wisdom. Any time you feel the tiniest twinge of doubt, give yourself time to check things out further. This applies to financial as well as relational choices. My sister quoted a phrase that has stuck with me: "When in doubt—don't."

These are some ways that I have learned to strengthen my own intuition:

    a. Learn to sense your emotions. This first strategy is going to sound like I am contradicting myself in the section above, but I am not. While we do not need to allow our emotions to run our decisions, we do need to tune into them.

Take time to notice the various emotions you have throughout the day. You don't have to wait until you have a strong feeling. We are all continually having emotions. Allow yourself to become aware of what you are feeling even when things are calm. This is what I have found to strengthen my intuition. Your intuition is connected to those subtle emotions, such as a twinge of doubt, a mild feeling of fear, caution, or dread. These can be warning signs that can save you much heartache.

    b. Practice mindfulness on a regular basis. You can literally train your brain to delay and restrain impulses and calm your emotions down through mindfulness. Just a small segment of time regularly can do more than you think.

Here is an example of how to engage in mindfulness:

Find a quiet place that is comfortable and feels safe from distractions. Rather than trying to empty your mind, do the opposite; fill up your awareness with everything you notice around you in the here-and-now moment. Begin to bring in the sights, colors, and images around you. Focus totally on them. Now, begin to include any sounds around you. If outdoors, there may be sounds of nature, and if indoors, you may notice just the sound of the air-conditioning or a faint cadence of what you hear from a separate room. Next, bring in any fragrances, preferably focusing on having pleasant scents around you. You could bring with you a pleasant aromatherapy resource before you begin. Draw that scent in now. You may also be able to imagine a memory of your most fragrant, soothing aroma in your mind. Now include tactile, kinesthetic, and even taste. You could bring a healthy beverage into the room.

Bring all these senses together into your awareness. Allow these images and experiences to fill up your mind, crowding out all other distractions.

Do this as often as is reasonable with your schedule. It may be as frequently as daily for five to ten minutes (or longer) or as little as monthly or weekly. As often as you can practice this, I believe you will find benefit. When you become adept at this skill, you can sometimes grab a minute or two of mindfulness at brief intervals in the middle of your schedule, as long as you are not driving or operating machinery.

4. Don't let yourself be manipulated.

I have found the most difficult purchase to resist was that of buying for someone I love, and I admit that I have been manipulated in this way. If someone is pressuring you to spend more money on them than is reasonable, this may provide an important test of their loyalty to you.

There is a story in Luke 15:11-32 (NIV) that describes a young man who asked his father for his part of the financial inheritance, so his father gave it to him. In an instant, this young lad was rich. He left home to seek life adventures, yet returned having learned some bigger life lessons. While he had a lot of money, he had people flocking to him as friends. He was popular and likely felt loved and valued by those showing him such enthusiastic attention.

Then, before he knew it, the money was gone. He had spent all of it on a lavish adventure. Once the money was gone, all these "friends" disappeared one by one as well. He returned home, now wiser, having learned the hard way. Here, he found forgiveness and true unconditional love from his father.

That friend who gives you those puppy-dog eyes if you are not in a position to buy that gift, dinner, or product for them may not truly be your friend. Those who really do care about you will not want you to overextend.

Some of us parents, if we did not have a lot of possessions while growing up, may be tempted to give our kids everything that we did not have. There is sometimes a tendency for parents to swing equally too far in the opposite direction, attempting to correct a wrong of the past. This is not a good solution; rather a balance somewhere between stringent and excessive can be found.

Teaching our kids to work for things they want, save their own hard-earned money, and delay gratification can build a deeper sense of appreciation and add strong character in them. There may be times to bless them with that awesome surprise and other times to let them feel the strength of earning their own rewards.

If you do not feel at peace making a purchase for someone and they visibly become sad or want you to feel guilty, give yourself a moment before giving in. Acquiescing to their wants might temporarily quieten the storm or tantrum or stop the flow of tears, only to find that the tears, rants, pouts, and tantrums become bigger and stronger at the next quest they seek from you. It is better to deal with the pouting or ranting now than to have this problem grow bigger.

Here is an amazing secret that I find many people, even full-grown mature adults, often don't realize. We do not have the power to cause that other person to feel what they are feeling. For instance, they get mad at you because you do not feel comfortable doing something that they want. You have not caused them to become angry with you. They are solely making themselves angry through the thoughts and beliefs that they are telling themselves in their own heads. They may want you to think that you caused their feelings. They may even believe that you caused them to feel that way. But that is not the truth. People generate their own feelings from their own beliefs, perceptions, and interpretations of what is happening.

Of course, there are events from which most of us may feel sad, hurt, or angry, but I am talking about the situation in which a manipulator may want to guilt you into giving in to their whims. This is different. For example, you say I need to save some money and make moderate rather than extravagant choices for a while. Person A may get mad and visibly pull back their attention to you until you give in. Person B may give a whole different response by saying that it is okay and helping you come up with some of those moderate choices. Same event, different outcome. Person A may tell themselves in their head that you are cheap or selfish or that this is a bad situation. These are thoughts they generate in their own head that lead them to feel angry or disappointed. Person B may think that they understand and want to spend time with you for you and not your money.

Their own thoughts lead them to feel calmness, possibly compassion, or maybe even grateful to you for your honesty.

5. Remind yourself of all the blessings you already have.

You may find that what you already have is exactly what you need. Train your mind to notice all of even the tiniest blessings you encounter throughout the day. Take time to notice positive features in yourself and in those you love. It is easy to become complacent with all the modern conveniences around you, yet if you stop and count them, you may find that you have more blessings than you realize.

Sometimes the familiar can become routine and seem to lose its sense of adventure or newness. Do not let this tendency rob you of seeing what you have. Notice the person with whom you are in a relationship. What first drew you to them? What are those quiet, sustainable qualities that they possess that a noisy, flamboyant person might attempt to drown out? Is your companion slow but steady? Are they not so patient but have a drive for getting things done? Remember the positive side of their personality that may have gotten overshadowed by years of familiarity. Revisit the first day you met and some of the past moments that had impressed you.

Sometimes people change. Perhaps lately those once-admired features rarely emerge to the surface. Perhaps they have experienced some events since you first got together that require healing. Look beneath the sparkle that may have dulled. You may see that your partner is a person who needs your patience and understanding. They may even need additional professional help. If their behavior has become extreme, there may need to be a different set of boundaries established if, in fact, safety and well-being have become challenged.

Ideally, marriage is a journey where two committed friends walk side by side through life's ups and downs, together, learning how to support each other. Every long-term couple I know has gone through some difficult periods during their time together. When they make it through these challenges, they often emerge on quiet seas, reaching a deeper and more solid foundation than ever before. Through any storms in life, take time to even make a list of those positive qualities in your partner that might have faded behind a cloud.

Any time we concentrate on deficits, we rob ourselves. When you choose to hyperfocus on your perceived annoyances of your partner, friends, family member, job, co-workers, and lack of belongings, you are filling your mind with a sense of scarcity while completely missing out on what *IS* right in front of you that you *DO* have *NOW*.

This strategy also applies to your own attitude toward yourself. If, in a given day, you only have energy to do one or two things, acknowledge and celebrate that thing you did accomplish rather than nag yourself about those things that you did not get done. Often, those other things can wait until tomorrow.

You have a choice to use your mind and intuition for what is best for you. Keep your eyes open, examine all options, and give yourself the time that you need. While aiming for the prize, don't let yourself miss out on the abundance that is already yours and is happening all around you right now!

Chapter Eight

Don't Be Afraid or Intimidated by Bullies

As I mentioned above, Kitty was a calm, mild-mannered cat. When she was in her prime, she was free to roam inside and outside at will. She mainly stayed indoors, but we gave her freedom to enjoy the neighborhood as well.

One day, we were out in the front yard with her. It was a bright spring day. The weather was warm and pleasant; the sun was shining. Kitty was sitting there at ease under our large Live Oak tree. Suddenly, a dog three times her size (much larger than Mack who you see in the picture above) came charging up to her, thinking that he was going to push her off her post. As he got closer and closer, he suddenly realized that she was not about to move nor even flinch. He pressed his paws forward on the ground and came to a screeching halt. He landed right in front of her, face-to-face, nose to nose. She just stared at him, eye to eye, with an undaunted, partially bored, and slightly annoyed look, as if to say, "What?!"

She stood her ground, appearing completely unfazed at his power move. The dog shrank down, relinquished his posture, and slinked away, never to be seen by us again. This cat lived twenty-one years, and I believe that one of the reasons for her longevity was that she was fearless and unintimidated.

This story about Kitty relates to strategies for dealing with bullies. I grew up not having a single clue about how to deal with intimidation, but my cat apparently had some wisdom. How do you deal with someone who picks on you? How do you deal with that person who tries to steal your lunch money, [friends, career, spouse, or reputation]?

I used to believe that if you are nice to the intimidator and appease them, then they will go away happy and leave you alone. This may work for people who understand tenderness and caring, but it may not work for those who do not. There are those people who may not have had such things even introduced or taught to them. Not only do they not know what to do with goodwill, but they may mistakenly view you as weak and perceive you as an easy target.

My upbringing taught me to show kindness and love to everyone. This does not typically work well with someone who wants to have power over you. In fact, the more of your power you give away to them, the more they may want from you. This book does not give you any guarantees or specific cookie-cutter solutions because every situation is different. Here are some options to consider and weigh out according to each unique situation:

Bullies: What You *CAN* Consider

1. There are times to avoid all contact with them completely.

This consideration is straight and to the point. If the person is truly dangerous, it is okay to avoid dealing with them altogether. There are times when it is smart to run or hide. Do not try to be a hero or outsmart them. Your welfare is much too important. There is no shame in avoiding a dangerous person.

2. You can choose to ignore them.

Sometimes the best response is no response, if they are not dangerous. If they are just looking for someone from whom to get a reaction, and you give them nothing, you are giving them no fodder. If they don't get a rise out of you, they may not find you an enjoyable target. This is a time when it is good to be perceived as boring—at least to a bully. They may move on to seek another possible quest, as I suppose that dog did in our yard that day.

Remember, just because someone tries to engage you, it does not mean that you owe them a response. Even if they are expecting an answer, you are not socially obligated. You may have given a response in the past, yet you can change the game rules, and this time ignore them, leaving them with nothing to work with from you. This can be considered a win on your part.

It is simple. If you don't water it, it cannot grow.

3. Don't take it personally.

In most cases, do not take personal offense if the bully is trying to insult you. The true saying applies here: What people do to you is more about them than it is about you. Someone who seeks a person to pick on usually has something going on inside them that drives them to inflict fear or harm on another person. They may need professional help. This is unfortunate, but it is not your job to be their therapist.

When you do realize that their choice of behavior may indicate a difficulty in their life, you are moving yourself into a more powerful position than that of being a victim. You do not have to know what that difficulty is, nor try to fix it. You can just consider what difficulties in their life might be motivating their cruel behavior, and you move into compassion. As you move your perspective in this manner, you move yourself emotionally out from under them and their power.

For many bullying situations, I recommend compassion from an emotional (and often physical) distance. In your concern for their plight, you can pray for them or wish for them a better situation. If you sense that they may become a danger to themselves or someone else, you can call 911 and alert someone in authority who can check out their situation further. These are times to get professionals involved.

When you turn your focus away from yourself and onto a bigger picture, it is now no longer about you and, therefore, not personal. This can free you up to move on to something entirely different from the situation completely.

4. Don't let them under your skin.

How do you ignore a relentless tormentor? How do you keep from letting them get to you? You may feel like you need to make them stop. Each time they make a jab at you—especially if they find your *really* sensitive emotional buttons—you may be giving them exactly what they want when you react. You may be feeding that big giant whale.

You do not have control over other people's choices and behaviors, but you *can* control YOU! This comes from what you do inside your own head without having to even speak a word out loud. How do you do this?

You can set boundaries, and in this case, emotional boundaries. First, let's talk about boundaries in general.

A boundary is a type of barrier that keeps unwanted things out. Yards have fences, buildings have walls and locked doors, and YOU get to have boundaries too! Physical boundaries involve the proximity of people around you. You may decide who can or cannot sit next to you or who can come visit you at your home. You also get to decide to spend time and how much time (temporal boundaries) to spend with a particular person.

Definitely, the letters N and O come into play here when you need to set a physical or temporal boundary. An example could be the following:

Someone says, "Do you want to go out to dinner with me?"

You say "No."

Another example could be: "Will you do this chore, task, homework, payment for me?"

You give the simple word, "No."

You can be polite and gentle about this, letting them know that you are not available due to work, school, or whatever you are doing. Nevertheless, we can learn to set physical, temporal, financial, and all other types of boundaries in our lives when we want to prevent exploitation. Your boundaries also include the privacy of your personal information, such as your history, your personal journal or diary, your health and medical records, your banking and other accounts, and any other information you deem private.

Your boundaries are to be respected. If you are under the authority of someone who is the one trying to cross a boundary of yours, you may very well need to seek help from a trusted person in charge. If you are younger than eighteen years of age, you may need to bring your concern to a parent or teacher. If this happens in the workplace, you may need to make a report to a higher manager and/or your human resources department.

So now let's talk about ways to prevent the bully from getting under your skin emotionally. This involves setting an emotional boundary. You can do this by choosing the thoughts that you put in your own mind. Yes, you do get to be the gatekeeper and author of the thoughts, attitudes, beliefs, perceptions, and interpretations that you choose to put into your own mind. We all need to learn the skill of choosing how we are going to interpret and mentally process a situation. Sometimes there are cases in which properly prescribed medication can help to make this task easier.

What if a bully is saying insults about you—even right up in your face? Even worse, what if they are disparaging someone you love? There are several ways to set these emotional boundaries. First, recognize that they do not get to be the authority over your value (nor your loved one's)—even if they think they are. With each retort coming from them during this encounter, tell yourself silently in your head a fact that can help you override their foolishness. One example is *That person does not have any authority over my (or my loved one's) worth*. Another is *That person does not get to determine my (or my loved one's) future*. Continue to focus your mind only on this overriding truth in your mind for the whole encounter. Don't let any of their words get past your ears. As soon as possible, remove yourself from them, shut the door, hang up the phone, leave the room, or drive away.

You can also choose to think thoughts that turn the situation around from it being about you to it being about the bully themself instead. This is applying what was mentioned about involving the truth that what people do to you is more about them than it is about you. While they are going off, making all that noise, and twisting themselves into a ridiculous fruit loop, you can silently tell yourself things like, "*Hmmm, I wonder what happened to them to make them want to act this way? WOW, they are really misled about this! No one gave them any authority about me or my life.*"

However, make sure to keep all these thoughts to yourself. It typically does not help to confront them. In fact, if you say some of these things out loud to them, they may escalate the situation because they are most likely looking for a fight. You are not their punching bag!

When I was twenty-six years old, I went through basic training in the United States Air Force. I had been hired as the female vocalist for the Texas Air National Guard 531st Band, and I had to pay my dues like everyone else. Now, no disrespect to the military training process, but as a therapist (before I even finished all the academic years of school), I did not approve of yelling at people. Basic training is designed to toughen people up so that they can survive on the battlefield if deployed.

Now, as a junior therapist in that environment, trying to help everyone long before I was trained or seasoned as a therapist, I found it hard to set emotional boundaries at times. When I saw a fellow trainee do a power grab and become bossy toward a peer, I would speak up to give them better ideas (unsolicited advice) on more respectful ways to talk to that person. This would be met with irritation and rejection. People who want power instead of pleasantness may not be interested in these suggestions.

On one particular day, however, I was able to set strong emotional boundaries. As part of the training process, the upper sergeants came into our barracks to do an inspection. As I look back, I know that this was part of the process to weed out individuals who may not be able to survive the rigors of military battle. I still disapproved of the yelling, though. So, these sergeants entered. We were all to stand at attention in front of our open lockers. They were allowed to search for anything that might be inappropriate among our possessions.

One by one, this group of four or five high-ranking sergeants clustered together and scrutinized the belongings of each recruit. If nothing stood out to them, they would all move on to team up together on the next soldier. All of us obediently standing at attention, facing straight ahead, could hear each encounter in the room. I remember one young woman, as they started to loudly grill her about some of her belongings, began to cry and ask for them to give her understanding. As they escalated, she began sobbing and begging them. I remember her words, "Please, sir." This did absolutely no good whatsoever for her. The more she sobbed, the more they pressured her. We all stood there in silence, some of us feeling compassion for her. This demonstrated that asking someone for mercy when they have no intention of giving it can be futile.

Finally, they came to my locker as I was toward the last of their excursions. A therapist in the making, about to be a professional singer for the military (rather than a war hero), I was really a fish out of water. I did not predict how strict basic training was, and as a kind of health nut at the time, my locker contained some herbs and vitamins, plus a Walkman radio cassette player, and my music jogging tape that I had brought with me. I had thought that in my spare time, I would be able to go jogging. I had no idea!

They had a field day with me! All of them teamed up on me. One higher-ranking man drilled me about my belongings. I continued to stay at attention and stare straight ahead, giving appropriate "Yes, sir, no, sir" responses. When he found out I had a psychology degree, he tried to taunt me with sarcasm, saying, "I have a psychology degree too! Do you want to sit in my office and discuss psychology?"

I remember replying some sort of affirmative—I knew no difference. At this point, his yelling became more intense. I continued to stay calm and not let anything he was yelling get to me. I don't remember what his last statement was, but by that time, his mouth was right next to my left ear as he yelled his last tirade.

I remember I was not influenced at all by what he was saying or how loud he was yelling. At his last attempt to get a reaction out of me other than the fitting "Yes, sir, no, sir," I do recall having a subtle smile in the corner of my eye as I did not allow him to impact me. At that last moment, I believe I filtered that event through a lens of humor in my mind, perceiving that he could not do anything to get to me. I was the triumphant victor—not him. I did not allow anything they said or did to penetrate my soul. They may have seen this, too, as they moved on and gave up on trying to get me to lose control.

After they left, some of the fellow trainees responded to me with amazement at how I kept my composure and made everything they did just roll off me.

This is an example of an emotional boundary. Just because someone is yelling at you or mocking you, you do not have to give them any power. Just because they might be saying things that are negative about you or those you love, no one has given them the authority. You can transform everything they are saying into nothingness. They have no power when you do not allow them to have emotional impact.

Also, a really fun strategy—yet it must remain private in your head—is the transformative perception. As you notice the amount of energy, time, effort, and emotional space they spend on you, a reframe is to think something like, *Wow, I must be really important in their mind for them to spend this much time and energy thinking about me! Hmmmm, I must be taking up a lot of real estate in their head and living rent-free!*

Now remember, these thoughts are just for you. Do not say them out loud. If I had said to that drill sergeant something like, "No, but I might let you schedule an appointment with me, in *my* office, after I finish my doctorate someday or autograph one of my future published books for you, if you are so lucky," it would not have gone well at all! In fact, my first published book on how to forgive dictates that I forgive him… which I have.

5. There are times to stand your ground.

There are cases in which you may need to be very strong and not allow bad behavior to slide. For reasonable people, who may have good intentions, this could be as simple as going to them and letting them know how their actions impacted you or your loved ones. These situations could result in simple conversations with many opportunities for healing and a positive outcome.

There are other cases in which the person is not likely to be reasonable. In this example, the person who committed the offense may respond with resistance or retaliation. These cases may require more courageous action from you, such as making an official report, filing a complaint, or using legal recourse.

Each situation is different, and some cases may require wise counsel before making a decision on how to approach the issue. It can be wise to prepare, seek wise guidance on your strategies of taking a stand, and plan for protection if it is needed.

Whether just a simple conversation or a formal legal process, it may feel very uncomfortable speaking up and taking a stand. You can weigh the decision based on risks versus benefits for yourself as well as others. Sometimes doing nothing allows the wrongdoing to continue hurting you and/or others. It would be nice if it were easy and the person to be confronted responded with a welcome mat, but it may not be the case.

When I was in elementary school, even kids would call each other tattletales. I wonder how this got to be labeled as bad. Is it okay to just let some people continue doing wrong in secret, getting away scot-free, and having absolutely no consequence? I believe the term "tattletale" was only invented to shame observers into silence and to help wrongdoers continue hurting the innocent.

In healthy work environments, there is often a non-retaliation policy. This is designed to prevent the person being reported from punishing the reporter. In companies in which I have worked, it did not matter how high you were up the ladder, you were not allowed to retaliate against the person reporting you in any way.

Whether to stand firm or walk away is a case-by-case decision. If you believe that you may want to take a stand for the good of someone or for an important cause, seek support and consult those with wisdom for guidance. Each case is different. Also, allow support from others rather than take anything on alone.

Sometimes this is a challenging process, and other times they may shrink down and avoid hassling you if they know that you are unstoppable. Their response is not easy to predict. However, it has often been said that many bullies are cowards. If they believe that their attempt to harm you may turn out to be detrimental to them, they may avoid you like the plague. This would be one situation in which it is preferable to be perceived as scary—at least to the bully. It is not easy to predict whether they will shrink back or retaliate, so use caution.

In summary, handling a bullying situation is a case-by-case decision process. It may be necessary to consult with someone you trust. Managing yourself first before attempting to manage the bully may benefit you well. This may involve physical and emotional boundary setting. At times, it may require showing no fear, as my cat did that day, or if they are dangerous, it can be smart just to run!

Chapter Nine

Choose What Is Good for You

Remember Myndie, my little mini pinscher, you see here perched up on her back legs, who started out as a stray? Well, from surviving on the streets, she had developed some habits—some of which I liked and others I needed to learn to understand. One of the most intriguing behaviors was her willingness to eat vegetables. In all my life, I had never seen a dog like this. Every time I put together a salad, she perched up on her back legs with full attention, eagerly ready to take—you name it—lettuce, cauliflower, carrots, green beans, and yes, even broccoli. She would quickly jump up and catch in her mouth whatever I would toss her way.

Even as I stood there chopping up lettuce and veggies, she would watch attentively. I would hand her a little piece of broccoli or cauliflower and say, "Do you want a little 'tree'?" She would snatch it so swiftly from me, I would have to be careful that she did not take my fingers along with it, too. Mack, seeing her enthusiasm for these things, automatically assumed that they must be good, and so, to this day, he loves carrots, green beans, and those little "trees."

How did Myndie acquire a liking for these veggies? Well, if you think about it, if you are a dog on the streets and have to find your dinner from the throw-outs, what are the most likely foods that people tend to discard and leave behind? You guessed it—salads and vegetables! I imagine that she, hungry and tired, foraged through the trash and came upon the rejects of the menu. The first bite of lettuce or carrot that entered her mouth may have filled her aching tummy and given her a huge sense of relief from her hunger. Soon, she likely began to associate broccoli and carrots with that sense of relief from her hunger and, more importantly, comfort and survival.

Rethink Your Perception of Vegetables and Fruits

What is your attitude toward healthy cuisine? Have you somehow associated vegetables with a category of food you consider boring? Do you consider these foods "have-tos" instead of "want-tos"? Many perceive vegetables as boring and see starchy, fatty foods as a comfort. Not Myndie. For her, veggies brought her comfort.

Traditional comfort foods such as creamy starches do not really bring us comfort. They may initially spike our energy, but they often contain too many sugars or carbs, both of which eventually send our energy plummeting back down into a crash. Carbs turn into sugars in our bodies, so both eventually bring us down. They may first provide an initial sense of comfort as the sugar effect enhances our mood in the short term, giving us immediate gratification. Healthy forms of protein are generally more stabilizing to our physical energy.

A negative perception associated with healthy nutrition often happens unintentionally by well-meaning loved ones. Sometimes, eating your vegetables can be conditioned in our minds as a chore or something to get through first before we can have the "pleasure." Dessert comes after we have consumed our nutrients. I would not reverse this because it is better to fill up on the healthy nutrients first. You can also have your healthy dessert later as a snack after lunch.

We can train ourselves to associate healthy nutrition with the good that it does provide. For instance, think of fruit. What is your favorite? Notice its vibrant color and its fresh juices bursting with flavor. Compare the way that your body feels after having fruit versus something creamy or sugary. You may notice a feeling of refreshed energy after a rich cup of fruit or berries. Think of the luscious flavor in watermelon, cantaloupe, pineapple, sweet orange slices, or a beautiful assortment of berries. Notice how they satisfy.

The same new awarenesses can be developed with salads. Many of the positive associations can be formed by the way salads are put together. Can this be a time of togetherness with your family or loved ones? This can even become a bonding experience with someone preparing the lettuce, another perhaps sweet kale, and another a choice of high-fiber ingredients.

When I was growing up, meals were not prepared in this way. This may have been the case for you, too. In my household, one person worked hard to get the meal on the table. They were rushed and pressured. During the meal, that same person sat nearest to the kitchen so they could get up and down from the table, running back and forth to get whatever anyone needed. Then, after the meal, they were tasked with cleaning up the kitchen by themselves. In other households, the mood at the table may flavor your relationship to nutrition. There may be silence so thick that you can hardly choke down a bite. In another, there may be arguments and strife. This does not pair well with good digestion. There may be some of us who did not have happy meal experiences, so the association with healthy nutrition is tainted with something negative.

If any of these examples are you, consider yourself not alone. Here is what is important: You get to make new rules and create your own healthy patterns for yourself. Don't let anything that happened in your past steal anything from you today. Create a good and healthy life for yourself now with all the opportunities you can find.

Ways to Recreate Your Perception of Healthy Cuisine

A salad can become a creation of ingredients you choose, resulting in a vibrant, colorful mixture of added condiments you can make to your liking. Notice the difference you may feel after consuming a nice salad with perhaps some nuts or berries, feta cheese or croutons—whatever you like. This is your own creation.

It is hard to make a mistake in creating a salad because you get to choose the ingredients that you like. You may feel lighter and less sluggish by including healthy nutrition in your repertoire of meals than if you only include meats, potatoes, and desserts.

Were some of the sweet or unhealthy foods associated with positive experiences for you? Sometimes we go out for ice cream with loved ones or share decadent slices of cake with friends. Sometimes people have found themselves becoming addicted to mind-altering substances because when engaging with them, they initially felt acceptance, belongingness, or emotional freedom.

For years, studies have shown a tendency for our brains to associate attachment of emotional needs with some forms of food or substances. This is because initially, while partaking, we may have been in a situation in which we were feeling loved, safe, or important. The way our brain works is that it begins to respond with that same feeling of warmth or inclusion just at the introduction of that substance, which is a counterfeit item. Our brain pairs the counterfeit item (sweets, snacks, or other substances) with that experience of being loved or accepted. Soon, that substance, all by itself (in the absence of that love experience), can bring on a positive feeling. It is now connected in our minds to that memory of the true love experience. This memory is more often implicit (a memory where the details of the event's origin are no longer clear) rather than explicit (a memory with clear details of that original experience). At times when love and acceptance feel absent, we may begin to consume that substitute item to eliminate feelings of loneliness, sadness, or depression. This is why some may find that just the thought of cheesecake, ice cream, or whatever that substance was, brings up a cheerful feeling within. The substance has absolutely no power to bring us that love or safety.

A solution is to learn again how to supply yourself with healthy attachments in the present and in your future. It can take time to regenerate the love and emotional connection (replacing the counterfeit substitute). True, healthy love is what can really satisfy the soul. In deciding to let go of that counterfeit substitute, there may be a period of grieving, yet that is part of healing. It can take time and a little trial and error, but it is worth it.

Rethink Your Perception of Exercise

I could barely put on my exercise shoes without Myndie rising up with excited expectation to go on a walk. All I had to say was, "Let's do the walk," and both Mack (who followed her cue) and Myndie were up and headed for the door. After getting their leashes on, Myndie would begin to jump as high as she could at the doorknob. Once I opened the door, she would yank on the leash, pushing her body forward with all her force, trying to pull me forward. Right there in the front yard, she would let out the loudest shriek, announcing to the world (and disturbing all the neighbors while at it) that we were on the move!

What I appreciated most in her was her gratitude and enthusiasm. All I had to do was say, "Wanna do the walk?" and she would become an animated bundle of exuberant joy.

How do you feel at the prospect of doing a walk? I'm guessing that for many of us, we have associated exercise with a dreaded chore. This association is not natural. When you were younger, perhaps in elementary school or kindergarten, what was the natural response when the teacher would say, "It's time for recess"?

Can you imagine all the kids throwing themselves down on their desks, saying, "Oh, no, not recess!" or "I want to keep sitting here"?

I remember when the recess bell rang, there was immediate newfound energy and enthusiasm in all the kids. With great excitement, all would run out to the playground to play ball, to swing, to climb, and to run around in the outdoors.

Whether you are grown or not yet grown, there is still a kid inside you that needs to get out and play. The gym, the jogging track, the exercise room—these are some of your playgrounds and can help keep you young. We will never outgrow the need for activity. Change the way you perceive exercise and find ways to move that are fun for you. There is dancing, golfing, bowling, hiking, weight lifting, and many other ways to keep yourself fit.

Take Good Care of Your Overall Health

For a number of years, Mack has had regular veterinary acupuncture appointments and other maintenance health care. Now that he is older, he receives shots for his joints. His food is selected from healthy brands of dog food. When he was younger, he would go on regular walks. Now, although he is older and the walks are shorter, he still has the energy of an adolescent dog at times. Although he does not move as fast as he did when young, he still feels like playing and can sprint up a couple of steps on the backyard patio.

We are never too young nor become too old to continue taking care of ourselves. Do all that you can to maintain your physical as well as mental health.

This can give you energy, strength, and well-being. You will also look better, too.

Choose Relationships That Are Good for You

Luke was a sweet dog we had for a few years. He would try to dig himself out to leave our yard. This was because my husband at the time had adopted him from a guy who was engaged and about to be married. The guy was giving the dog away only because his fiancée apparently wanted him to do so. From what I was told, the guy's fiancée did not have any particular medical condition or allergic issue in connection with the dog. It appeared that she just did not want to have a dog in their lives. I could be wrong. There may have been a different reason, but not from what I learned when he was brought to us.

I was not present when my husband at the time went to their home to take him. From what it sounded like, even now, the more I think about it, the guy's fiancée may have given him an ultimatum: "It's either the dog or me. Perhaps the guy had been pressured to prove his level of commitment to this new partner by acquiescing to her demand to give up the dog. I was told that the guy had tears in his eyes as he handed Luke over. If I had been more assertive back then, I would have given the dog back to that guy.

Most of us tend to ignore telltale warning signs in a person. Don't kick yourself if you have done this. I don't believe that it indicates any foolishness on your part; you may just be a generous person who gives hope, trust, and abundant chances to people in your life. Sometimes we do not heed warning signs because we do not want to think that someone would really have a bad intention or be that selfish. So we give them the benefit of the doubt until our patience finally runs out.

During the budding stages of a relationship, allow yourself to see some of the hints given to you along the way. Notice any discrepancies. Do they say one thing and then do another? How do they treat other people whom they perceive as less powerful or less important than themselves? How do they deal with constructive criticism? Do they make excuses, blame others (or you), or even turn it around on you? Do they give you an explanation that leaves your gut (intuition) feeling or thinking, "Hmmmm, that doesn't fit"?

Alternatively, do they genuinely show appreciation for your life dreams, goals, and aspirations? (Do you also appreciate theirs?) How do they really behave when you begin to embark upon the long, arduous road of those achievements? Do they put you in a position to choose them over this dream? Do they create a competition between your love for them and your love for anything or anyone else precious to you, as if you cannot have both?

Sometimes people simply need to grow in their maturity. In these cases, you may be able to address some of these issues and see a sincere change in their behavior. Other times, these events can be hints and suggestions of a possible deeply ingrained characterological pattern that the person may not want to change.

Take your time in selecting long-term partnerships. If someone does not respect your need to take a reasonable amount of time in getting to know them before becoming serious in the relationship, this could also be a red flag. If someone is pressuring you to hurry and make that commitment and ignoring the fact that you are not ready, ask yourself a question. Could this be a pattern?

Give it time. You may want to make sure that they will not try to railroad you or disregard your feelings or needs about other matters in the future. Anything pressured or rushed may have warning flags inherent within.

The moral of the story about Luke is that if someone tries to force you into an ultimatum between them versus the dog, it may be a sign to choose the dog. But never forget that *YOU* are the prize.

Chapter Ten

Don't Be Afraid to Try Again—to Love Again

Angel was a beautiful Dalmatian that we did not have for very long. When she was just a little puppy, she would melt your heart with just one look. She would let me cuddle her like a baby and was one of the sweetest dogs I have ever had. From her story, I believe a more appropriate term to generalize all our pets could be "fur angels" because so many of them are like sweet little angels in a coat of fur.

This is the one dog with my biggest regret. I had completely entrusted her care to an adult who lived in the household at the time while I was working and in graduate school. I could not have imagined that anyone would mistreat her or mistreat any pet, for that matter. This adult claimed to know a lot about animals and to really like dogs.

It happened when she was no longer a puppy yet still young enough to be energetic. She had apparently felt a great deal of anxiety one day, and she took her comforter out of her dog house and shredded it all over the backyard. Rather than attempt to see what was going on with her needs at the time, the entrusted adult became enraged at her and mistreated her. Next thing I knew, after coming home one day, she was not in the backyard. I was told that she had run away. I did not question this person at the time since they seemed trustworthy.

Not too much time passed when I was in the front part of the house and heard something at the front door. I opened it and there she stood, leaning slightly to the side and appearing apologetic. I immediately dropped to the floor and wrapped my arms completely around her. I held her for a very long time.

My very first fur angel and first "pet-love" was my childhood dog. He was specifically chosen for me to help reduce my asthma symptoms. He was a little black chihuahua with bright perky eyes that I named Skipper. I remember as clear as day when my father brought him home for me. He was the tiniest little guy, sitting right there in the palm of my dad's hand. It was instant love at first sight. Skipper lived a good life, being the center of my attention and my world, for approximately the next decade. As I think about it, I do not recall having to have those frequent ER asthma treatments that I had previously required since he came into our home. It was not until years later, after he had passed away, that I remember having a severe asthma attack.

Skipper became my personal companion. The bond was mutual, and I spent most of my free time with him after school from elementary age through middle school. He seemed to be comfortable with all of my mothering attention to him. When I was little, I would carry him around wrapped in a blanket as if he were my baby. He would just lie there, snuggled in my arms, just going with it. He didn't seem to mind at all.

Back in those days, dogs were allowed to roam the neighborhoods. There were no leash laws, nor did they have to stay confined in a fenced yard. Since Skipper would sometimes go out and readily come back, this became a normal routine. He did not tend to stay gone very long, except for one particular day.

I was still in elementary school when this happened. Skipper had been let out in the front yard as normal, but it had been days, and he had not returned home. I was so upset and worried that I retreated to my room and began to cry. I sobbed until evening, and when my father came home from work, he came and sat down on the edge of my bed. I recall him encouraging me not to worry and saying these exact words, "We'll find him tomorrow."

Those definite words stood out, and I had heard them without skepticism or question. He did not say, "We *may* find him tomorrow" or "We'll look for him tomorrow." He said, "We'll *find* him tomorrow."

This was quite a bold statement. How could he know? What was the likelihood of it really happening tomorrow? It had already been days. I trusted my parents without hesitation. His soft-spoken words dried my tears and gave me hope. My father was good at providing comfort. He was a peaceful and gentle man who did not flaunt religion yet prayed with sincerity and lived with honest integrity.

The next day, after school, I came home and decided to look down that one alley that I had missed. As I approached, I saw a truck parked in the middle of the alleyway. There were dogs everywhere. This was the house where a female dog lived, who Skipper apparently claimed as his girlfriend. It seemed that all the other dogs in the neighborhood had the same idea and were competing for her attention.

I had never seen a dog pound or even its truck before, but had heard stories about them. They pick up dogs, and if you don't go and get them from the pound or cannot pay their fees, it is not a happy ending.

I asked the man in the truck if he had seen a black chihuahua and gave him specific descriptions of Skipper. Lo and behold, he opened the back of his truck and unlocked one of the cages, and there he was, about to be taken away forever! I had found him on the "tomorrow" my dad had asserted, and just in the nick of time!

The guy released Skipper to me—no fines, no fees, no resistance. I carried him home in my arms. The statement my father had said came to pass, not necessarily as *"we"* will find him, but he was found. Any minute later, and it would have been too late, as he was already in the dog pound cage.

While my mother was nurturing, it was my dad who was the one who comforted me and spent quality time with me. He came home from work that day to find a very happy and thankful child.

This, my first childhood dog, was my first deep attachment to any of our pets. He was irreplaceable. He also had a unique sensitivity for the feelings of those around him. This became clearly apparent later when I was in the sixth grade.

Skipper unexplainably became suddenly sick for a couple of days and stained the carpets throughout our home. Right after those two days, when my forty-three-year-old father was away, he unexpectedly had a fatal heart attack that took him immediately. Skipper's symptoms then abruptly stopped, as if he had been deeply struggling with his sense of an impending tragedy.

I was eleven years old when this happened, and in one single instant, my whole world was shattered. The whole family was in shock and became disrupted.

For the next several years, I watched my mother grieve. I remember being awakened during the night as she got up and down, unable to sleep and unable to stop crying. Somehow, my tendency toward sound sleep had paled. She never burdened us children with this. She just suffered in silence.

As an intuitive child, I walked with my mother through her next several years of deep loneliness. He had been the love of her life, her high school sweetheart, and her soulmate. They had just recently had their 25th wedding anniversary, and at the end of their date that evening, she had just told him how she wanted twenty-five more years.

The shock of this experience shook my perspective for several years to come. All at once, it appeared to me that happiness and bliss could suddenly be snatched away, destroyed in an instant, without warning and for no reason at all. Moreover, my mother's happiness had abruptly plunged into a deep abyss of aloneness and our whole family system was changed overnight.

After that happened, I could not understand why a person would fall in love. It did not make sense to make a lifelong investment in a great marriage partner, only to have them suddenly pass away. It felt as if life had crashed into a brick wall without warning.

Because of this, for years, I placed a barrier over my heart. During my younger years, I selected dates and partners who were not right for me. Alternatively, sometimes, while even younger, I would develop crushes only on those who were out of my reach. These strategies were unconscious efforts to ensure that I would not find a perfect match or soul mate, allowing me to avoid the risk of having my heart abandoned and broken again.

This avoidance turned out to cost me more greatly than I realized at the time. The cauterization of my heart translated over into my future pets for several years as well. I definitely took good care of, nurtured, and loved each and every one of them, but I limited my level of attachment to them. This was because I feared the pain of someday letting go, given their short life spans. It was not until Mack, who you see on the front cover of this book, that I began to reopen my heart again for these little fur angels who can bring us such joy.

The deepest opening of my heart, however, happened in my thirties at the point of becoming a mother. It was then that I truly began to understand the profound depth and breadth that love can reach into every dimension of a person's soul.

* * *

It is very hard to put love in your heart if it is filled with pain. All of us can be faced with the loss of someone precious to us, yet few may know how to grieve. Yet even fewer may know how to comfort those left behind. There are often no words, no magical phrases that can fix the situation or bring that loved one back. Perhaps only when they are ready can a glimmer of hope be introduced.

The first lesson of how to love again—to try again—may involve specific strategies to heal your heart. I have learned some ways that may help you.

Dealing with Grief

This is my absolutely least favorite feeling—sadness. Let's face it. Hurt *hurts!* There are times when we need to grieve the loss of a person or pet, and other times we need to grieve the loss of the dream—the expectation of how it was supposed to go, yet didn't. We cannot get rid of pain with addictions to substances, obsessions, video gaming, overworking, or substitute loves to try to fill in that wide, gaping wound. This just delays our healing. The irritating irony is that to get rid of grief, we need to grieve. The process requires *feeling* it. *Ugh!* Such a counterintuitive paradox! The good news is that you do not have to feel it all at once, so keep reading.

As a trained clinician in psychological trauma and also a human being who has walked through grief, I believe I can show you some ways to get through it and come out alive. There is a term used in trauma work called "pacing and containing." This means that *YOU* get to set the pace of your grieving.

Just like any major project at school or work, this task, grief, is to be processed a little bit at a time. No great work was accomplished overnight. Even God took six days to create everything, and then… what did he do on the seventh day? He RESTED! This pacing and containing thing has been a necessary process from the beginning of time. If even the Creator rested, who am I to be exempt from needing a break from painful work? So, you get to come up for air in the middle of your grief.

To Grieve or Not to Grieve

Even though you may think you are fine, if you are avoiding the process of grieving your emotions, you may be keeping your body in a state of fight-or-flight. This sends stress hormones throughout your body and wears and tears on your vital organs. Attempting to be placid on the outside, you may be running an exhaustion chamber on the inside, which can lead to health problems.

How to Grieve

I believe that feeling all the grief all at once is retraumatizing. Also, one of the biggest fears about grief is that it will become overwhelming and take over your whole life. It does not have to be this way.

First, give yourself a specific timeframe for focusing on the grieving. Now you are managing it rather than it managing you. You can literally decide that on such and such a day, once (or twice) per week, you are going to devote ten or twenty minutes to your emotions on this loss. You may want to have with you a journal (or a trusted friend, competent therapist, etc.) and spend time letting out some of those feelings.

In 1969 Elisabeth Kübler-Ross identified five stages of grief. The emotional processes between the stages of shock/numbness (the typical starting point) and acceptance (the typical resolution point) involve sadness, anger, and bargaining. Each of the stages are not processed in any exact order. Let's take a look at these three areas.

Sadness

When you are grieving, do not take yourself into despair. This means keep your intensity level of sadness at a moderate level. Here is how you do this. Pay attention to the thoughts that you are telling yourself in your head while you are grieving. Make sure that your thoughts toward yourself and the situation are *only* thoughts of comfort. *Absolutely* make sure that your thoughts are not blaming or shaming yourself. Also, make sure you are not telling yourself gloom and doom thoughts while you grieve—or ever, for that matter. All your thoughts need to be realistic yet reassuring and soothing.

The intensity level of sadness needs to remain moderate and not extreme. Extreme intensity of sadness (despair) is not healthy for you, and it is not productive. It is worth saying it again: absolutely refrain from shaming or blaming yourself in your head. Yes, you *can* change your thoughts. It may be helpful to have a therapist or a wise, supportive friend with you when you grieve to help you steer away from self-shame and self-blame.

This can take some practice, but you can learn this important skill. Telling yourself supportive thoughts in your head is very important. No one has the power over the day of death (Ecclesiastes 8:8). We may have some decision on a date of euthanasia for our pets and/or other instances in other countries. However, we generally may not have ultimate power over the events that may lead to this decision. We cannot control the universe, so give yourself mercy and compassion.

Examples of ways to give this gentleness to yourself involve telling yourself what you *did* do right. It is important for you to remind yourself of those times you did show kindness to that loved one. Indeed, I believe that this loved one you are grieving, and who cares for you, would not likely want to see you left behind in torment over mistakes or regrets, not if they do love you like you loved them.

<u>Anger</u>

Anger can be perceived as a very negative emotion. Anger in and of itself is not negative—it is what we choose to do with it that can be okay or not okay. Understanding anger and its purpose is important.

At its root, anger is energy designed to repair. This is the reason that it is part of grief. There is something that went wrong and logically merits repair. However, it is often something that we cannot mend, reverse, or fix. We cannot bring that loved one back nor make that person change their mind. So we have energy stored up with no place to go except either stuffed into our body, or vented out of our body, as it should be released.

Anger is also to be managed and kept at a moderate level of intensity. If it is too intense, we experience rage, which is also not helpful nor healthy. You can process the anger in tolerable doses for short lengths of time and find substantial relief.

A few ways to get that energy released are through physical movement. Some people take a walk, go to the gym, or have a good run. You can express your feelings when hitting a baseball, throwing balls of clay at a distant board, or yelling into a pillow. You can achieve a great deal of relief by talking about the issue with a trusted friend or therapist. Some people have told me that they let themselves scream in the privacy of their car. You can set up a safe and private place that does not involve any harm to person or property, and get those feelings out of your body in a constructive manner. This is energy to be released.

Remember to keep the intensity at a moderate level and the time short so that you do not overwhelm or trigger yourself. It can be very helpful to have an understanding friend with you for support.

At any point at which you feel the temptation to lose control, stop, take a deep breath, and acknowledge that you have processed enough anger for the time being. This is the point to redirect your energy into a calming, soothing, restful activity. Tell yourself that you have done a very good job of processing the amount of anger that needed to be released for now. In pacing and containing, it is important to set the rest aside for later. Just like that major project at school or work or developing strength at the gym, this is to be done a little bit at a time for true healing and growth.

<u>Bargaining</u>

This involves the "Why" questions and the "If only" statements. While connecting with sadness, shedding tears, or expressing anger, you may feel the need to ask these "why" questions. It is okay to voice what is on your heart. Sometimes we get mad at God. Again, if anger is energy designed to repair, it involves energy directed toward understanding something or debating what happened. If you are mad at that person for dying or mad at God because something was allowed to happen, it does not indicate disrespect toward them. It is basically energy involving your expectation of something that did not transpire. It actually means that you have a relationship with them and expected something different from them. The level of your anger may be a reflection of the level of love and expectation toward that person or that yearning. This is energy that can (and should) be directed into a constructive outlet.

In healthy relationships, it is permissible to ask for understanding. Through the bargaining stage, this may be your intention—to understand. You were created as an intelligent being. Therefore, seeking to understand cannot be wrong. To my authorities and elders, of course, if I ask them "Why?," I always ask with an attitude of respect. Using the words "How come?" or "Help me understand" can often come across as more respectful than using the word "Why?"

Give yourself time to process your grief. Allow as much time as you need, and don't worry about how long it takes for you. Your length of time for healing is unique. You do get to have some decisiveness in this timetable.

Additional Ways to Grieve

As I mentioned, sadness is my least favorite process. Back when I was a child, and my whole family lost my father, none of us knew how to grieve, so I believe several of us in the family just stuffed the pain down in our hearts. This became a mess. Later, since I still did not like grieving but had learned how to process those emotions, I sometimes elected to grieve in advance.

For instance, regarding the entrusted adult in my house mentioned above, I began to open my eyes about him. As this happened, I began to grieve the death of the marriage far before it happened. This actually prepared me for the eventual separation and dissolution of the relationship that I ended up initiating. If you find that a person to whom you have opened your heart has betrayed you and it does not seem reparable, you can grieve in advance, like I did, which can prepare your heart to move forward. Indeed, I believe that better blessings are awaiting you ahead in your life.

Sometimes, if you know that a loss is impending, you can begin to process some of your grief emotions proactively. Also, in many cases, the benefit of having advanced notice of an impending loss can give you the chance to devote special time and attention to that loved one or pet who is ill. This awareness can be a gift.

We Do Not Outgrow the Need to Grieve

In my professional work, I have taught many people how to overcome trauma, heal, and forgive.[2] I have learned how to rise above a wide range of hurtful events. Regardless of how skilled you become at coping with difficult events, no one ever becomes exempt from needing to grieve at times. You can be the king or queen of mental health and wellness, yet you are still human. Others whom we love are also human and may sometimes behave in unexpected ways, whether intentionally or not.

Recently, I encountered a situation with someone I love dearly. I understood many of the underlying dynamics and

---

[2] Dr. Joan Weathersbee Ellason. *Finally… the how to of Forgiveness: A three-tier approach to dry your tears*. Oasis Workshops with Dr. Joan Weathersbee Ellason, 2020. www.drjwe.com

possible reasons for the way the situation turned out. Still, I had deeply hoped for it to go much differently. It didn't.

After the encounter, I used all the cognitive tools that I had previously learned for healthy coping. I did everything I knew to do the "rising above" process that I teach. Yet, even having good, solid coping skills, I noticed that I was still feeling bothered and thinking about the event. As I sat there, I felt a bit dizzy. Curious, I dug out the old blood pressure cuff and put it on my arm. To my astonishment, the reading was higher than I had ever had in my life (179 over 87 and my heart rate of 64 beats per minute). I attempted to relax and took my blood pressure again several times, but it was still abnormally high. This physical symptom seemed to be happening under the surface and having a life of its own beyond my control.

I realized that even though I had done all the cognitive work on what had happened, I was still suppressing the emotional pain. I had learned a long time ago that stuffing painful feelings can lead to medical issues. There was no way that I was going to let this happen. I did not want to allow it to fester inside me. Above all, I did not want someone I cared for to (unintentionally) be able to have any impact on me in this way.

I knew that I needed to practice what I had been preaching. I needed to grieve. Not long after that, while sitting in the privacy of my office chair, I made the effort to allow myself to connect with the sadness and hurt. As I moved the business of the day aside, my thoughts and interpretations of the event that had felt painful began to come to the surface. In the safety of solitude, little by little, the tears began to flow. I allowed myself to connect with the sadness in order to get rid of it. Soon, I began to sob, weeping openly and expressing aloud my disappointment.

Mack stopped what he was doing and walked over to me. I saw him looking up at me, so I reached down to pet him. He then moved closer to me, aligning the side of his body to my right leg and pressing in as if to give support and comfort.

Even though I wanted to grieve without a person seeing or hearing, it was okay for Mack to be in the room. Our pets can give comfort without judgment when we sometimes do not want others to see or know the depth of our pain or how much they hurt us. I am thankful to still have him here with me in his old age.

I allowed myself to reach deep down inside, pull up those painful feelings, and eject them out of my body. Not long after, I rechecked my blood pressure. It had gone back down to 120 over 72 with 77 beats per minute.

Treasuring the Gifts While They Are Present

Pouring some of your love and energy into someone you treasure is not wasted. We do not know how long we can have them in our lives. Rather than regret what you shoulda, coulda, woulda done for that loved one or pet after they have gone, right now, make a list of things you can do for them while they are still here with you. You can choose to fulfill those kindnesses and acts of appreciation now while you still have them.

Dealing with loss can turn us into wiser friends, partners, and pet parents. After some healing from my childhood loss of my father, I began to approach love differently than before. I decided to treat every relationship – the ones important to me - with a deep respect. I had learned to not waste any of the limited time given. Each relationship that is important to me, I make an effort to make every moment count, not waste time on trivial annoyances (as with all humans, there are plenty of them), and to treasure every aspect worth appreciating in that person. You can learn to appreciate the precious time with those in your life *while they are here* and not fret so much over their imperfections.

Why Take the Risk?

After surviving a negative relationship, we are given choices:

1. Remain stuck in its negative residue, or

2. Learn something, change, and make a better life.

I choose the latter. Do not allow yourself to stay stuck in past mistakes. You can actually turn a past regret into a springboard toward triumph.

Even the negative relationships that I experienced provided me with something that I would not have otherwise had. Now, I am not advising you to fearlessly plunge headlong into any relationship that has warning signs. If you did come out of a negative experience, however, there can be benefits. Those that I walked through gave me the impetus to become more courageous, more determined, and more resolute than I believe I would have been if I had not experienced them. If you have been through a negative experience, you are likely now to be wiser, braver, and stronger than you were before.

The benefits of a healthy relationship far outweigh the deficits. With a best friend by your side, you can have companionship for a number of activities. You can have someone to just sit and be silent with as you enjoy the day or evening. After teaching your partner how to understand and respond to your needs (and you theirs), you may have someone to lean on and confide in during hard times. You may not enjoy the same interests, yet you can add new dimensions to each other's experience *with* those differences.

Couples with healthy interactions tend to be healthier emotionally as well as physically.

How to Embark Wisely

You don't have to be afraid to try again. All the way through the opportunity set before you, you have options. You can slow down the pace, giving yourself more time to know more about that person. If they do not show very much patience to allow you a reasonable amount of latitude, this itself is information for you. If they are not willing to consider your needs or your pace early on, what might that mean about them in the long run? Does it paint a picture of how your life might be with them? Would this possibly be a life of you having to sacrifice your own needs for theirs excessively?

There are those, on the other hand, who are willing to allow you to teach them about your needs. It is important to teach your partner how to treat you. Inform them about your needs and your boundaries, so that you do not lose yourself in the relationship. It is not all about them, nor is it all about you, but it can be all inclusive—about you both as a couple and as individuals. Communicating with each other about your needs and theirs has to be a mutual endeavor.

Teaching people in our lives to honor our needs and respect our boundaries creates a healthy balance. As you are starting a new relationship, there may also be some important personal goals and needs, such as school aspirations, personal hobbies, spending time alone to recharge, or other important activities that replenish you. Beginning to teach those you love that you also need time to carve out these recharging activities for yourself is fair to both of you. You both get to create a relationship pattern that includes time together as well as healthy time separately. This balance promotes longevity in the relationship. You have a bond with each other, yet you also both have some legitimate and healthy outside interests. When you come back together, you have new things to discuss and share.

If and when you decide to reopen your heart, you can give yourself freedom. You can give yourself the freedom to be in charge of how fast the relationship develops by listening to your own heart. Do not ignore your intuition or any questions arising if things don't seem to add up. Check out any assumptions and questions that feel puzzling.

Sometimes we hang on too long. You can give yourself permission to change plans right in the middle of the process if you need to do so. This may spare others also from heartache that might have occurred down the road. Contrary to some retail transactions, it is never too late to ask for a refund or an exchange.

Springing Back from a Negative Experience

After my first negative relationship, which was much earlier in my life, I learned to go completely in the opposite direction from my former timid, self-effacing, acquiescent nature. I became brave, decided to learn how to be assertive, and began to use it. With this assertiveness, I also took singing lessons and learned to walk out on stage before a huge crowd and belt out a song that could give inspiration to a coliseum-sized audience with no shyness whatsoever.

If it weren't for what I decided to do with this negative experience, I likely would not have my doctorate today because I would likely have remained that timid and shy person, waiting for others to take care of me. The negative experience in my early twenties woke me up and led to my taking a 180^0 turn in my life. This transformed into a springboard for me to push beyond what I knew. I also became a better counselor in the future, helping others push through and beyond their plight.

Making Room for the Little Fur Angels

There are so many ways that love offers itself to us and brings an opportunity for blessings. Often, it comes through those little beings we adopt as pets. Here are a few accounts of such gifts that those little pets can bring.

Dr. Joan Weathersbee Ellason

A Cat-astrophic Tale

My best friend from college described some unexpected events when they were moving from Texas to halfway across the country. Her husband had a new career opportunity and needed to get the whole family moved in time to start his new position. All packed up and almost ready to go, they discovered a small litter of cats that had been abandoned in the alley behind their house. This was a busy alley, and it was clear that they would be in danger if left there.

They searched for and called the nearby pet stores and even contacted a benevolent animal company, which they thought could take in stray cats. One by one, each of these organizations turned them down. Finally, not wanting to leave the kittens stranded nor jeopardize his career by arriving late, they decided to take all four kittens with them on the long drive across four states to their destination.

Now they already had some cats of their own. So they packed up their own cats with these four new ones. The four new female kittens included, as later named, Cali, Houdini (Dini), Smokey (Cujo), and Ninja. They made room for them in their fully packed Tahoe with their original three cats—two females named Fluffy and Princess, and a male named Gizmo. The whole family spent the next seventeen hours cramped in their vehicle listening to a seven-cat chorus of "meow... meow... meow..." all the way there. Well, almost seven... Princess, their gray tabby, was the only one who did not join the feline opera. She sat right up in the front seat during the trip as if she were completely comfortable with the long journey.

They finally made it to their destination. As they settled into their new home, their search for pet adopters did not stop. They also made sure that each of the new kittens had proper veterinary care. After they got settled, they started displaying the cats, and a lady showed much interest in all of them. As the woman drew close to the litter, Cujo took down the whole enterprise in a swipe of her single paw. Immediately, the lady backed off and was not having *any* of them. The deal was off! So at that point, they just completely threw in the towel on trying to find good homes for them and kept all four new baby cats.

As the years went by, it became clear in several ways that keeping all of them was going to turn out to be fortuitous. One of these kittens provided unexpected companionship for my friend. When she was younger, she had a very beloved cat named Spot. Spot was a calico, named as such because of a spotted pattern on one side of her face. Spot had died of cancer years ago when my friend was younger.

So, as it turned out, one of these little kittens she named Cali Rose happened to have the same unique spotted pattern on her face as her former beloved Spot. Inexplicably, this was the only one of the litter that followed my friend everywhere in the house that she went. It almost seemed to her like a restoration of that earlier connection and relationship she had adored with Spot.

Moreover, each of the cats had their own unique personality and gift they brought to the family. They nicknamed one of the calicos Houdini because she would disappear and hide. They would finally find her perched in the window, watching all of them while they were busy looking for her.

In fact, as they look back now, they can see some specific, unique blessings that came from each one. Each cat had their own different personality and skill set. One was extra nurturing to the others and could dash in a flash to protect the group. This one they named Ninja. She was sweet and constantly cleaning the other cats. Another playful one, they named Smokey, was nicknamed Cujo because, as her personality developed, she was both fearful and a defender and named after the Stephen King book.[3]

Not long after this, the totally unprecedented pandemic of 2020 mandated that everyone in America stay sheltered in their homes unless their work required otherwise. This isolation proved to be difficult for so many. Loneliness and depression abounded in some households. Others, if not trapped between four walls with a dysfunctional family member, at least suffered with boredom for many months on end. During this time, for my friend and her family, these cats all turned out to be nonstop entertainment. Watching them all run at each other and play with the arched back and banter kept their days lively and filled with fun while they had to be cooped up. In retrospect, they are glad that they kept them.

<u>A Tale of Comfort</u>

"Sheeba, a small black half cocker spaniel and chow chow, brought a unique blessing in my life when I was troubled. I would sit in the backyard and simply talk and pray as I petted her. As she cuddled up against me, she gave me the comfort I needed. And I could always count on her to

---

[3] Stephen King. *Cujo*. FisicalBook, 2011.

not tell a soul!" (Judy K. Melton, my sister, personal communication, August 22, 2025).

Rescued by the Rescued

A neighbor, on the 49th anniversary of her marriage, reluctantly gave in to her husband's persistent request to take in an 8-week-old rescue dog. This was a dog who did not seem to fit anywhere, had no specific breed, and was classified as just a mutt. When asked what breed she was, she described her as part Red Heeler and part Jack Russell terrier, but just plain *MUTT!* This neighbor and her husband named her LuElen.

Unexpectedly, in 2021, her husband of almost fifty years passed away. She stated, "If I had not agreed to my husband wanting to adopt LuElen on our 49th anniversary, I would not be comforted by her companionship after he passed away . . . God blessed me with my husband and the eight-week-old puppy he chose for us." (Colma Cole, personal communication, August 22, 2025).

When the Unexpected Becomes Meant to Be

You never know what unexpected blessings can come in an unlikely encounter. Another story comes from a colleague of mine.

"Adopting Riley proved to be the best unintentional decision or 'accident' of my life. Who would've thought that a 48-pound mixed black lab puppy would so easily seize my heart? Not I. I have had three examples of unblemished love. The first two were my grandmother's. Riley became the third. I consider our bond one of life's greatest bounties. For true love can never be purchased or stolen. True love comes from an eternal source, and if we are touched enough to experience it even once in our lives, we are indeed rich beyond measure." (Jason Branson, personal communication, August 22, 2025).

Opening Your Heart

Angel was willing to try again. What a brave and loving dog! I will never forget her.

The lessons of love and loss may first involve wisdom in your choice of that person or pet whom you bring into your life. There are also strategies and ways to enhance the success of this love attachment and relationship. The most challenging is if we, in fact, come to a time of having to release them from our hands. This part of the task might seem illogical or frustrating. Why love if you might have to someday let them go?

Here is what I have learned. If you avoid love, refuse to sometimes risk trust, and shield yourself from connection, you cheat yourself out of a wealth of richness and blessing in your life. You could elect to stay with what amounts to low investment and feels safe to you, choosing to close your heart off from love and trust, thereby pretty much guaranteeing yourself what is predictably an empty vacuum. If you choose, you can have a life of nothing—no risk of attachment from opening yourself—and you may most likely look back, having played it safe, to find your hands empty. I also believe that without taking some wise risks, you and I very well may miss our calling and our destiny on this Earth. If I had never encountered the task of grieving the loss of my dad, I would not have become a counselor.

Life has so many unexpected twists and turns. No matter how the loss happens, it is never easy to let go of anyone you love. Allowing oneself to open their heart to love involves unknowns with respect to both pets and people. I have walked through both avoidance and grief and have learned that love is worth the risk.

Here is a great paradox. If we go through life avoiding pain, we can very well end up creating more pain for ourselves. Embarking on a relationship journey can have inherent risks, since we do not control others or know the future. No one can guarantee a happy outcome, yet there are ways to make our choices carefully and thoughtfully. We can learn wisdom to increase the chances of a positive road ahead.

You Get to Choose Who to Let In

As mentioned above, take time to get to know the people that you are considering for your inner circle of close friends and confidants. Notice how they treat others, especially those (who they perceive to be) in a less powerful position than they are.

Another way to learn about their behavioral patterns can be to learn about the family system in which they were raised. This is not always readily forthcoming, and the information may come gradually. Again, give these things time. Anything worth the choice of a life partner deserves patience.

When learning about the person's family system, take your time to look beyond the exterior. Sometimes a person is raised in a dysfunctional family system, yet they have made a resolute decision to manage their future family in a much healthier manner. They may have been inspired by that one grandparent or that one healthy mentor who provided them with a whole different perspective on how to treat those they love.

Keep your eyes and ears open for signs, behaviors, or hints that may show a contradiction between what is said and what is actually done. Don't hesitate to notice this information, and don't sweep these cues under the rug. You can either make a mental note and see what happens further, or you can speak up to check out your impressions.

While feeling emotions with your heart, keep your head at the very top of your decisions. This may be very challenging because, as you begin to feel attached, you may be tempted to make excuses for them or deny what your head is telling you. *Listen to your head as well as your heart!* This may spare you pain later.

Be Loving & Forgiving to Yourself If You Discover You Made a Wrong Choice

Even if you spent substantial time and did everything by the book, don't be hard on yourself if you discover something you missed about the person. This is planet Earth, so everyone is human and nothing is perfect. Sometimes we get hurt by the ones we trusted, and there are also times when people change.

If you come across surprises, give yourself permission and the realization that you are not all-knowing and did the best you could. Also, remember, if you gave trust and the other person botched it, you are the generous one, and they have been foolish with your generosity. You gave them a chance to be in partnership with you. You have been a generous donor.

An example I often use is that of a loving parent wanting to bless their young son or daughter. The young driver just got their license, and the parent just acquired a fancy new car. By giving the keys with the strict guideline to only take it carefully around the block, the parent offers an opportunity for a blessing to their teen. The teen takes the keys, revs the engine, races it outside the boundaries of their agreement, and damages the car. Who is the foolish one? It was the person who chose to disregard the needs and requests of the one who was generous. The parent offered an opportunity and did not say, "Now, wreck the car."

If you offered someone trust and they botched it, you are not the fool. Their behavior was foolish, and you had generously given them a great opportunity—a relationship with you! Your heart can heal, and cars can be fixed. In the final analysis, they lose—you do not.

It is hoped that this book will give you some tools and strategies to help you walk through the unknown, to overcome, to rise above, and to conquer many of the traumas in life. This is so that you may have a full, rich life filled with all the opportunities and blessings that it has to offer you.

Love Comes in Many Forms

There are many stretches of highway on which we are single and do not see the prospect of a partner in sight. This is not a deficit. Allow yourself the wealth of rich friendships. I have learned to be content both while married and while single. You do not have to be lonely if you do not have a soul mate. You can find much joy in a wide range of friendships around you.

Even more importantly, and likely the most neglected area, is your own relationship with yourself. How are you treating yourself? Do you tune in to your needs and supply them in constructive, healthy ways? What are your thoughts that you are telling yourself in your head all day long? Are they constructive and supportive? Are they loving? Even without a spouse, partner, or many friends, it is important for you to love yourself and be your own best friend as well. If you are pouring love and gentleness into your soul, then you have love and kindness to reach in and pour out onto others.

In fact, the first step of finding healthy love outside is to cultivate it within ourselves. If we treat ourselves poorly, we teach others that it is okay to treat us poorly. If we treat ourselves with respect, we send a message to potential friends and companions that we are to be respected.

Making Room in Our Hearts

Making room for loved ones in our hearts, both people and those sweet little fur angels, can give us an abundance that surpasses imagination. You can take time to heal and gradually allow yourself to notice the opportunity for new possibilities around you as you become ready. Be loving and gentle with yourself during this process.

Even if some of these blessings do not last as long as we wish, you do get to keep their memory and the immense river of treasure that they pour into your heart and into your life. At the end of doing so, you will have a wealth of warmth and love to savor that no one on Earth can ever take away. This reservoir of love and wealth can remain with you in your heart forever.

Don't be afraid to try again—to love again. You can give yourself choices and options all along the way and go in with your eyes fully open. We learn from past experiences and become better at discernment.

Rise up out of the ashes, dust yourself off, and use all that energy designed to repair (the anger stage of grief mentioned above) to propel yourself into a transformation that you may have never thought possible.

www.ingramcontent.com/pod-product-compliance
Lightning Source LLC
Chambersburg PA
CBHW071852070526
44583CB00016B/1649